CASTLES IN WALES

LLYFR RICHARD A BETHAN YW HWN

CASTLES
IN WALES

GERALD MORGAN

First impression: 2008

© Gerald Morgan & Y Lolfa Cyf., 2008

Photographs courtesy of the author unless noted otherwise

The publisher acknowledges the financial support
of the Welsh Books Council

Cover design: Y Lolfa

ISBN: 9781847710314

Printed on acid-free and partly recycled paper
and published and bound in Wales by
Y Lolfa Cyf., Talybont, Ceredigion SY24 5AP
e-mail ylolfa@ylolfa.com
website www.ylolfa.com
tel 01970 832 304
fax 832 782

Contents

FOREWORD

THIS BOOK is intended as a pocket guide to as many interesting and visitable medieval castles in Wales as it was possible to squeeze in – some eighty altogether. There is an introduction for the general reader and an appended list, with one line per entry, of four hundred medieval Welsh castles and some doubtful claimants. The individual descriptions have three parts: Access, History and Buildings. My wish is to enthuse potential visitors, so I have spent more time on access than is usual, having visited every castle. I hope thus to overcome such obstacles as lack of signage, and sometimes attention is drawn to other attractions in the vicinity. Several entries contain more than one castle, e.g. the Three Castles of Gwent and the Gower Castles. Sections on history are generally longer than those on describing the buildings, because not much can be said in the space available about the complex developments at individual sites. There is a brief general guide to castle features in the Introduction. For the serious student the major castles have excellent published guides.

Naturally there are drawbacks. A full account of the castles which played their part in the history of Wales would include castles now in England; Welsh princes captured castles in England, while the invaders of Wales were based at castles at Gloucester, Hereford, Shrewsbury and Chester. Earthworks which are on private land away from roads are not described, but can be found listed in Appendix A, which attempts to list all the castles of Wales; enthusiasts will find ways of getting permission. A number of ruins usually called 'castles' have not been included, since they are better described as 'fortified manor houses' or tower houses, nor are the follies of the modern period such as Penrhyn or Gwrych castles. I particularly hope to interest people in the lesser-known castles well worth seeing, many of which are open to the public without charge (e.g. Llansteffan, Ewloe, Dolforwyn, the Three Castles of Gwent) and to the less-visited castles such as Caldicot, Usk, Kidwelly and Cilgerran. While the Edwardian castles of north Wales are widely known and have World Heritage status, the south has equally splendid castles less well-known: Cardiff, Caerphilly, Chepstow and Raglan are surely deserving of equal attention. Several obscure or difficult sites are reluctantly omitted, e.g. Carndochan and Dinas Emrys. Radnorshire is poorly represented because of its many castles, only two which are accessible – New Radnor and Painscastle – could be of any interest to a non-specialist.

No doubt some choices and omissions will cause surprise, but perfection is not to be achieved in this field. Equally contentious may be the decision to describe and list all sites according to the thirteen historical counties of Wales rather than the current unitary authorities, whose overall pattern I believe has not yet rooted itself in public awareness.

The castle-lover will often find it possible to visit several castles in a day, sometimes without having to spend one penny in entrance fees. The Three Castles of Gwent (Grosmont, Skenfrith and White Castle, all free) are a well-known example, treated together below. There are many such trios and pairs, among them: Ewloe, Flint and Caergwrle; Denbigh and Rhuddlan; Caernarfon and Beaumaris; Harlech and Cricieth; Montgomery and Dolforwyn; Castell Carreg Cennen, Dinefwr and Dryslwyn; Coity, Newcastle Bridgend and Ogmore; and numerous combinations in Pembrokeshire and the lordship of Gower.

Wheelchair users will find many castles difficult, some impossible, including most of the castles of the Welsh princes on account of their sites. Others have ramps provided where feasible, but spiral staircases in towers are clearly not negotiable. For information on disabled access to individual castles, contact the castle or local tourist information in advance. The *Cadw Guide for Disabled Visitors* is available online at www.cadw.wales.gov.uk. For general opening times and contact details for Cadw sites, also see www.cadw.wales.gov.uk.

I would like to thank Professor J Beverley Smith, Dr Llinos Beverley Smith and Dr Craig Owen Jones for offering much valuable criticism of the Introduction. Dr John Davies, Llandysul, kindly provided me with much information about building stones. The staff of the Royal Commission on Ancient and Historic Monuments Wales were most helpful, as were the staff of the National Library of Wales, the Castle Hotel, Ruthin and the Castle Hotel, Brecon. My thanks particularly to Cadw, Diane Mort and Deiniol Morgan for pictorial assistance, and above all to Lefi Gruffudd and Gwen Davies of Gwasg y Lolfa.

INTRODUCTION

What is a Castle?[1]

The word 'castle' conjures up a rainbow of ideas. Massive, ivy-covered, crumbling stone ruins can still be found occasionally, but they are fewer in number than they once were, since so many have been made secure and had most of their vegetation stripped away. We may think of the extraordinary pinnacles of the great Rhineland and Austrian fantasies, not so much practical fortifications as dreamtowers in Gondor, recreated on a small scale at Castell Coch, near Cardiff. Or, since the only French word for castle is *château*, the wonderful palaces of the Loire valley also hover in the imagination, though they were more palaces or mansions than fortresses, models for many a great country house in Britain. Beyond them in time and space are the huge Roman forts of the Saxon Shore, the fortifications of Byzantium and the great Crusader fortresses in Palestine.

More prosaically, medieval castles have traditionally been seen as overwhelmingly military in function, with their moats, drawbridges, battlements, portcullises, murder-holes and arrowslits, and there is truth in this concept. Recently however, castle scholars have reviewed the whole function of castles. While acknowledging that they were often symbols both of military aggression and defence, now their political and social significance is emphasised. In other words, castles were built as demonstrations of governance, prestige and wealth by kings and barons in competition with one another, and were designed to impress subjects, potential enemies, rivals and friendly visitors with a sense of magnificence and power. Not only was the castle important as a building complex, it was intimately related to the landscape which it dominated, as well as to the ego of its builder.

The simplest definition of a castle for the purposes of this book is 'a medieval European fortified stronghold', the word 'castle' deriving from Latin *castellum*, a small camp. Unfortunately the very name can be misleading. For example, 'castle' doesn't always mean 'castle' in terms of that definition. Maiden Castle in Dorset is a magnificent Iron Age fortified earthwork, with a Roman camp added in one corner, while Cyfarthfa Castle at Merthyr Tudful is the nineteenth-century creation of an ironmaster; neither place was a medieval stronghold. Nor are the equivalent Welsh words always helpful. Thus *caer* in Welsh place-names often refers to a Roman camp, but has other meanings, including 'castle', while *castell* was borrowed from Latin to denote a wide range of features: Castell Nadolig is an Iron Age hill-fort in Ceredigion, and Castell-y-gwynt a natural rock feature in the mountains of

Late Roman fortification: the Theodosian wall at Constantinople/Istanbul.

Snowdonia. What historians call 'fortified mansion houses' are sometimes popularly known as castles, but are largely beyond the scope of this book, though they certainly shared in the power-landscape agenda.

The Romans built what we may recognise as castles, especially the forts of the Saxon shore around the south-east coast of England; they also fortified towns like Caerwent. The Byzantine armies who briefly held north Africa in the sixth century AD also built stone fortresses which we would readily call castles. In Wales, even before the Normans came, there were defended strongholds, for which the place-name *dinas* or *din* was used, as at Dinas Powys and Dinas Emrys. But the

The classic Tump Terret motte at Trelleck, near Monmouth.

medieval castle as we know it in Britain emerged in ninth- and tenth-century France, when conditions had become sufficiently settled for local lords to build high mounds of packed earth or mottes, crowned with a wooden dwelling for the lord, and the whole encircled by a ditch and bank. Soon the embanked ditch enclosed land at the foot of the motte, this being the bailey or ward. Early in the eleventh century, several French lords built the first stone keeps or central towers since late Roman times, and the French pattern of the private (and sometimes royal) stone fortress spread into Normandy and over western Europe and through the Mediterranean to the Holy Land, reaching Wales after the conquest of England by the Normans.

That explanation may seem over-simple, and indeed it is. For a start, the form of castle known as a ringwork (bank, ditch and bailey but no motte) seems to have developed in pre-Norman England. The distinction between fortified manor houses, tower houses and castles is not easy; the categories can be ambiguous. Then there are the Welsh bishops' palaces. What is sometimes called Llandaff castle was actually the bishop of Llandaff's walled palace. Three more such palaces survive, built by bishops of St David's; all these buildings are the work of bishops fulfilling their rôle as Marcher lords. Other church buildings of castellated appearance or attribution include the magnificent Ewenny priory precinct walls, the Prior's Tower on Caldey Island and other tower-houses (mostly in the south-west). Apart from the bishop's castle-palace at Llawhaden, none of these sites is described in the main section of this book, though a few examples are listed in Appendix B. Many boroughs had castellated town walls around them, like those surviving at Conwy, Caernarfon and less substantially at Tenby.

The Meaning of Welsh Castles

In the English landscape, although there are many castles, the most iconic buildings are parish churches and country mansions, symbolic of peace and governance. In much of Wales, on the other hand, the truly iconic buildings are castles, symbolic of foreign occupation and native resistance, whose crumbling ruins eventually became romantic archetypes in dramatic landscapes. The Normans did not need as many castles in their rapid conquest of an already united England as they did in fragmented Wales, which could never have been subjugated without them. From the first, moreover, the Normans built castles for display and prestige; they should not be viewed simply as military fortresses – they were far more than that. They were centres of power certainly, the power of administration, both of law and order and of taxation, as well as centres of cultural exchange and diffusion.

A domestic fireplace in Kidwelly castle.

They did not need to be used in offence, nor very often in defence, except on the Scottish and Welsh frontiers where they are much commoner than in the rest of England and a good deal of Wales. It should also be remembered that castles were homes, providing domestic accommodation for lords, their families and their retainers. In the lord's frequent absence a constable was usually in charge.

Sovereign England had been effectively conquered with the death of King Harold at Hastings in 1066. Sovereignty in Wales, on the other hand, was divided; the land could only be swallowed up bit by bit. Conquest was only achieved by frequent bouts of local warfare over more than two centuries, culminating in several major royal campaigns. In this piecemeal process the castle was an essential weapon. To the Normans and the English that they became, their castles in Wales gave a feeling, often unjustified, of physical protection, and were ideal administrative, domestic and cultural centres in an alien and often hostile environment. To the Welsh they must often have seemed alarming and brutal intrusions, symbols of oppression, colonisation and acculturation, but in self-defence the Welsh learnt to build and use castles for their own purposes. Other Welshmen quickly understood the benefits to be gained by collaboration with the invaders. Many of Edward I's conquering soldiers of 1276–77, 1282–3 and 1294–5 were Welshmen. In 1277, for example, the trusted constable of Edward I's new and important castle at Builth was a Welshman, Hywel ap Meurig, who well knew which side of his bread was buttered.

Today, visitors to Wales are glad to admire the mighty castles of the great Marcher lords at Chepstow, Pembroke, Kidwelly, Raglan and Caerphilly, or the magnificent chain of royal castles in north Wales. Such is the splendour of their architecture, so outspoken is their apparent military function, that it is not easy to appreciate that these two groups were built for complex reasons. The massive castles of the Marcher lords were important not only for quelling the Welsh but for proclaiming each lord's status as a great magnate in rivalry with other magnates, while the Edwardian castles of the north were intended firstly to cow the independent-minded Welsh of Gwynedd into accepting their destiny as a conquered people, but secondly to protect new and alien boroughs; thirdly to serve as centres of administration, and finally to proclaim Edward's imperial and Arthurian status at the head of his English empire. It is noteworthy that at several of his castles, Edward had the hall timbers of the nearest Welsh court incorporated into the building.

Some visitors may prefer to visit the smaller but dramatically-sited castles built hither and yon by Welsh princes to defend their lands, whether in the Tywi valley at Carreg Cennen and Dinefwr, or in the north at Dolbadarn, Dolwyddelan, Dolforwyn and Dinas Brân. To the modern Welsh viewer, these may appear iconic of Welsh independence, of the remarkable processes by which several talented military leaders had learnt the tactics and methods of their mighty opponents, so that they could hold out for two centuries against looming conquest. But there are other Welsh-built castles too, now only earthen mounds or piles of stone (like Castell Meredydd near Machen in south-east Wales) which represent the survival of Welsh lordship in the midst of Anglo-Norman colonisation. These 'castles of the Welsh' were not only built as defences against the English, but by princes in rivalry with one another. Thus in 1156, Rhys ap Gruffudd ('the Lord Rhys') built a castle on the south bank of the Dyfi to remind the princes of Gwynedd that they no longer held sway south of the river as they had previously done.

The Hidden Narratives

There are however other hidden stories within all these castles. Both Marcher lords and Welsh princes exacted taxes and forced labour for their building; all castles shared this common narrative. They could only be created and sustained by enormous expenditure and effort. They were not simply weapons of shelter, prestige, conquest, defence and colonisation; they represent huge investments of craftsmanship, taxes and sweated labour. Nor does this apply

The Aberystwyth Old Castle ringwork.
Crown copyright RCAHMW.

only to the minority of castles built in stone; account must be made of the large number of castle mounds, banks and ditches which still survive, outside the remit of the tourist and heritage industries.

These lowly earthworks, not the mighty castles of Edward I, William Marshal or Gilbert de Clare, form the great majority of castles in Wales. Each has its significance. Even when a motte or ringwork has no documented history, even if we have no idea who built it, garrisoned it or stormed it, every such site represents part of that ebb and flow of conquest, reconquest and compromise which is the great political, cultural and military narrative of Welsh history from 1067 until the extinction of Owain Glyndŵr's rebellion early in the fifteenth century. The local historian who looks at the nearest motte with insight will have questions to ask: why was this spot chosen? What processes are here represented? What area did it control? What did its existence imply for the local population of the time? To what larger centre did it owe allegiance in the pecking order of the day? Is there a church nearby, and if so, which may have come first, church or castle, or could they be contemporaneous? Is there possible continuity between a castle and a local gentry mansion?

To medieval populations, therefore, the building of a castle had all kinds of implications: a change of ruler, forced labour for the peasantry, obligatory feeding of the imported craftsmen and the soldiers who guarded the site, not to mention their camp-followers. Local timber and eventually stone would be exploited, rents and taxes enforced. Settlement would begin around the new building, and might eventually become a borough. Fraternisation between local women and the newcomers would have the usual impact on the population. Social and physical landscapes changed. This is most obvious in the case of the many new boroughs established by the Crown, by Marcher lords and, in a few cases, by Welsh princes. The best-known of these are the royal walled boroughs of Conwy and Caernarfon, intended as deliberate plantations of English colonists with an implied economic and cultural mission to exploit the supposedly backward Welsh. Sufficient English settlers could not be found for all the new boroughs so Aberystwyth, for example, had a mixed Welsh–English population from the start. Craftsmen were needed: builders, armourers, blacksmiths, grooms to service the garrison, merchants to supply food and other necessaries. For the royal castles they were brought from all over England.

Another narrative invisible to the casual viewer of castles is their significance in cultural and linguistic change. We may like to think of the Lord Rhys spitting defiance from the ramparts of his castles at Dinefwr and Cardigan, or imagine the menace to the Welsh of William de Braose at Brecon. But these and other leaders were men of culture as well as war; they sometimes fought each other ferociously and could do unspeakable things to hostages and even to their own relatives, but they also married each other's daughters, attended each other's feasts and listened to each other's stories. It took the imagination of a Welsh dramatist, Saunders Lewis, to evoke a picture of the court of Llywelyn the Great at Aber near Bangor in the early thirteenth century. Llywelyn had married Joan (in Welsh, Siwan), daughter of John, king of England. Illegitimate she may have been, barely in her teens, but she was sent as a princess to the Welsh prince with a large train of French and English-speaking attendants, which must have had a dramatic impact on the manners, attitudes and speech of the native Welsh court. Even when in 1230, Llywelyn hanged William de Braose for sleeping with Joan, the marriage which the two magnates had arranged between Llywelyn's son and William's daughter went ahead. *Realpolitik* ruled. It was in this Cambro-French-English-Latin milieu that the great figure of Arthur the giant-slayer passed from Welsh legend to European literature and pseudo-history. In two Arthurian tales, one English and one Welsh, Arthurian narrative is located not at Caerleon, as so often, but at Cardiff, an obvious location for cultural exchange.[2]

Building Castles in Wales: Sites and Materials

The reasons for choosing a castle site may be obvious to us or may seem obscure. Simple choices involved re-use of an Iron Age hill-fort (Pen-rhos in Cardiganshire), a Roman fort (Cardiff, Loughor, Tomen-y-mur, Caerleon, Caerwent), or an early medieval fortification (Dinas Emrys, Carew), taking advantage of existing banks and ditches. Some clearly involved control of a roadway or river crossing. The Norman invaders

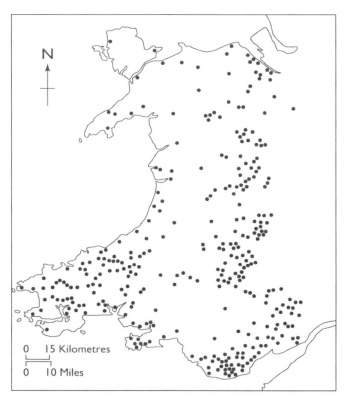

*The distribution of earthwork castles (mottes and ringworks)
in Wales. Cadw: Crown Copyright.*

sought control of the richer lowland areas, but always chose
sites safe from flooding. Where possible they exploited rivers
and springs to provide wet moats. They penetrated valleys or
moved along the southern coast, creating chains of castles each
offering refuge on a route as well as a statement of conquering
intent. Others were natural centres for controlling a newly

conquered area, becoming the administrative and economic centre of the lordship. Edward I demanded access by sea in every practicable case for ease of reinforcing and revictualling when besieged. In contrast, the most notable castles of the Welsh princes were perched on high crags, from Dinas Brân and Dolwyddelan to Carreg Cennen and Dinefwr; they were defensible, and commanded views over crucial valleys and mountain passes.

Several sites chosen by the Normans for castles have powerful significance in Welsh culture and legend. Narberth (Pembrokeshire) is the site commemorated in the beginning of the First Branch of the Mabinogion, the wonderful series of medieval Welsh tales, while Tomen-y-mur (Merionethshire) is the site of the court of Lleu Llaw Gyffes, hero of the Fourth Branch. It would be safe to assume that these Norman choices of legendary sites were coincidental. In the case of Caernarfon, however, it seems clear that its iconic nature, especially its Roman connections both real and legendary, influenced Edward I to choose it for his greatest castle and major centre of rule in north Wales, eventually preferring it to his original choice of Conwy.

Building Castles: Mottes and Ringworks

The vast majority of early castles in Wales were earth mottes, large mounds of soil and stones quickly thrown up by forced local labour, usually with a bailey or ward, i.e. an area at the foot of the mound defended by a bank. Most surviving Welsh castle mottes have been so eroded, abused and overgrown that many are only shadows of the steep mounds originally raised not only to protect their creators but to overawe the local peasants who did the actual excavating and earthmoving. Many have disappeared; among the best survivors are Wiston, Tomen y Rhodwydd, Sycharth and the motte at Cardiff.

The massive keep-tower at Pembroke.

The ringwork pattern was also used. Ringworks would contain a timber hall and other buildings, while mottes would be crowned with a timber keep and have other buildings in the bailey. The origin of the ringwork as an alternative to the motte is obscure, but they were built in England in the eleventh century and soon spread into Wales. Only in Glamorgan do they outnumber mottes, by 27 to 16; in the other twelve historic counties they are only frequent in Pembrokeshire (16), while in the rest, the totals vary from zero to seven, far outnumbered by mottes.[3] Various explanations for the distribution of ringworks in Wales are offered by scholars, in particular the differing geology of the countryside, but they are not always convincing. It may be suggested that a site on a ridge may have seemed particularly suitable for a ringwork. The majority of earth castles never developed beyond the timber stage, but the Normans gradually applied their stone-building techniques to a number of sites. Sometimes earth castles were developed in stone, other castles were stone from their beginnings.

Building Castles: Stone

The development of stone buildings in Norman Wales is a matter of much interest, since no stone building survives from the pre-Norman period. It seems that the Welsh had no interest in or tradition of building in stone, except by way of defensive banks. This cannot have been for lack of models; pre-Norman church architecture in England would have been known to the Welsh, while massive Roman ruins in stone survived on several sites in Wales itself. The lack of early Welsh stone buildings may perhaps be attributed to the primitive nature of the economy, or to the fissile politics of the times; in any case, timber and earth banking – set on stone foundations – seems to have satisfied pre-Norman Welsh needs.

The glorious arcade of Swansea castle.

As for building, timber and soil were easily available everywhere for raising mottes and ringworks. Stone was a more complicated matter. Most of Wales is well supplied with either limestone, sandstone or tough grits for wall-building and infilling, and the vast quantity of stone needed for walling meant that local stone was always used. Dressing stone for doors and windows was a different matter, since many local stones are unsuitable for carving. A number of Welsh quarries produced adequate dressing stone: Sudbrook in Gwent, Quarella and Sutton (both near Bridgend), Pwntan in south Cardiganshire, Egryn freestone in Merionethshire, Anglesey grits, Cefn sandstone, Cefnybedw and Holling rock (Flintshire) and Brycheiniog sandstones. The Normans however brought much of their dressing stone from England: to north Wales from Cheshire, to mid-Wales from Grinshill (Shropshire) and to south Wales from Dundry near Bristol.

Castle architecture is a difficult subject even for specialists; only a sketch is possible here. Basic problems are firstly the difficulty of dating; secondly, frequent additions and alterations; thirdly, the general degradation of buildings over five centuries or more, and finally the shortage of documentation, except in the case of the Edwardian castles. For the general public, the most obvious points of interest are castle plans and the interpretation of remaining buildings and fragments. Scholars deal in the often difficult and disputed field of influences from England and the rest of northern Europe which are beyond the scope of this small book.

Castle plans obviously depend on the situation available to the original builders. Mottes and ringworks could be built anywhere where there was sufficient depth of soil to create the necessary mounds, banks and ditches. Later builders in stone often had the choice either of adding to an original motte or ringwork, as at Caldicot and Builth, or of choosing a fresh site, as at Montgomery and Dolforwyn. Much then depended on the builders' resources; Welsh lords and princes were less wealthy than the Crown and the greatest Marcher lords. Some castles came into existence almost fully formed, so to speak (Conwy, Rhuddlan) while others were developed over centuries by successive owners (Chepstow, Cardiff).

The fundamental elements of castle planning and building in stone are: the exploitation of natural features; the choice of dominant building elements and style; the complexity of the entrance; the multiplication of turrets; the use where practicable of water features, whether natural or artificial, or both; and the standard of private accommodation. Some major castle-historians have argued for the logical development over time of keeps, towers and gatehouses in terms of increasing military sophistication and complexity, but the story is not so simple.

The garderobe (latrine) outlet at Dolforwyn.

Recognition of castle features is sometimes easy, sometimes not. Keeps, gates, towers and curtain walls are readily recognisable. Buildings and foundations within the walls are another matter. Sometimes the foundations only exist in bare stone outline, which would usually have supported timber buildings. In other cases there is plenty of walling, perhaps surviving to a first- or even second-floor level. What is difficult for the visitor to imagine is that what seems to be, for example, a hall, is actually the ground-level basement, with the hall itself reached by stairs to the first floor. Indeed it is a general rule that indoor life was to a considerable extent pursued on the first floor. Stone castles had chapels, but chapels are not always easily identified unless a piscina (a niche for washing communion vessels) or an east window survives. Features such as kitchens and ovens can often be recognised, as can the ubiquitous wells, fireplaces and garde-robes or latrines, placed on the outside of towers where the sewage simply fell down the outside walls.

The Invisible Castle

The term 'invisible castle' conveys all those features, obvious enough to contemporaries, that rarely or never survive. Nevertheless they must not be forgotten, for they remind us that these buildings were domestic residences. These bare, ruined interiors were once plastered and painted, with ceilings (long fallen in), and furniture suited to the rank of the chief occupant and the tastes of his wife. There were smells of cooking food, horses and stagnant moats, the sounds of dogs and blacksmith's hammers. Mass was said daily in the chapel or chapels – Caernarfon had five. There could be gardens within the larger castles, like Queen Eleanor's lawns at Rhuddlan and Caernarfon, or outside the walls, as remembered by Gerald of Wales at Manorbier. More than gardens, there were often deer parks, as at Raglan, fishponds, orchards, rabbit-breeding mounds, dovecotes, watermills, paddocks for horses and cattle, huts to accommodate the men and women who tended all these features. It is easier to imagine these features at Raglan or Cardiff than at a humble motte, yet Iolo Goch's famous poem to Owain Glyndŵr in praise of earth-and-timber Sycharth shows that these features were not confined to the greatest establishments. The castle landscape was not so much military as economic, and in Robert Liddiard's term, 'seigneurial'. Hunting, hawking and jousting were favoured entertainments. The extended castle landscape was a display of civilisation, representing man's control of God's creation, as against the wilderness beyond, and would have given delight to its landscaper.

As for the worship of God, chapels served only the castle-dwellers. Various arrangements were made for the boroughs attached to the castle. At Cardigan, Kidwelly and Chepstow, local Benedictine priories were founded, with substantial churches. Other boroughs might already be close to a long-

The chapel at Kidwelly; to the left the piscina for the sacred vessels, on the right, the sedilia or seats for the priests. The floor has long fallen in.

established Welsh church. Thus at Aberystwyth, the burgesses were expected to traipse over a mile to Llanbadarn Fawr and at Caernarfon to Llanbeblig, though in both cases, chapels were eventually provided within the boroughs.

The Military and Political Background

The Welsh existed as a separate people prior to the arrival of the Normans, but Wales was not a sovereign kingdom like England. Instead, Wales was divided into small units: the smallest was the commote, while two or three commotes formed a *cantref*, and a number of *cantrefi* might form a *gwlad* or small kingdom.

This gives a falsely mathematical impression; in fact, much depended on the capabilities of local rulers, who might rise from apparent obscurity to rule large areas, only for this unity to collapse at their deaths, since their chosen heirs were so frequently murdered or mutilated by family rivals. Different areas had their own royal dynasties, the most important of which were those of Gwynedd in the north-west, Powys in the east and Deheubarth in the south-west. But there were many lesser dynasties, especially in south and east Wales, several of which survived into the thirteenth century. Each petty king had one or more courts (*llysoedd*), where he accommodated his followers, administered justice and received tribute and taxes. The sites of many of them are known, but only one has been excavated and its stone foundations revealed, at Rhosyr (Newborough) in Anglesey.

From the English cities of Gloucester, Hereford, Shrewsbury and Chester, the new Norman lords set out with royal encouragement to conquer realms for themselves in the lands of Wales. They penetrated the valleys of the Wye, the Severn, the Usk, the Dee, and along the north and south coasts. So long as these men were personally loyal to the Crown, successive English kings did not hold them back; it was easy to reward their loyalty at the expense of the Welsh. Because there was no single ruler in Wales, the task may have seemed easy in prospect, since local forces of lightly-armed Welshmen were no match for the better-armed incomers in open combat, nor had the Welsh ever built castles to defend themselves. Indeed, by 1090, Wales had apparently been overwhelmed, but the Welsh came to see that guerrilla tactics were more effective than set battles. As Gerald of Wales perceived in the twelfth century, the invaders could not easily conquer a people who would 'never draw up its forces to engage an enemy army in the field, and will never allow itself to be besieged inside fortified

The Normans built their first Welsh castle at the lowest bridging point on the Wye, Chepstow.

strong-points'. The invaders, however, could hardly survive in potentially hostile territory without defensible refuges. For much of this period, the Welsh preferred to destroy castles rather than besiege and occupy them.

It seems clear in retrospect that Wales would not be conquered, unless the king of England decided to mount a major campaign while calling on his vassals to attack from more than one direction. English kings could, when not harassed by other difficulties, muster greater resources than the Welsh princes, and overwhelmed them in 1114, 1211, 1241, 1246 and the three Edwardian wars (1276–77, 1282–83, 1294–95). But kings of England usually had too many problems on their hands to concentrate everything on the difficulties of Wales. Thus the Welsh regained ground in 1094, in 1136, in 1165, in 1215 and 1257, culminating in 1267 with Henry III's recognition of Llywelyn ap Gruffudd as Prince of Wales.

The years between 1067, when William fitzOsbern began to build the first castle in Wales at Chepstow, and the final conquest of 1283, were a period of frequent but not constant fighting. Indeed, a good deal of the strife was among the different Welsh princes, who were sometimes willing to call on the help of the Crown or Marcher lords to defeat their Welsh enemies. Nevertheless, not all was bloodshed. Welsh princes pursued policies of alliance and intermarriage as well as battle. Not only did they marry each other's children, they married into Marcher families and brought off two marriages with English royalty. Dafydd ab Owain of Gwynedd married Henry II's sister Emma, and we have already told of the marriage of Llywelyn the Great and Joan, daughter of King John.

It is therefore too simplistic to regard the period 1067–1283 as one of absolute Welsh hostility to the colonising invaders. There was intermarriage, there was collaboration, there was imitation – indeed, there was deep cultural penetration, well illustrated in the person of Gerald of Wales, offspring of both Welsh princes and Marcher lords. In religion, in literature, in law and administration, Welsh traditions and practices were reformed and transformed. Above all, for our purposes, the Anglo-Norman revolution in Wales was set in stone – the stones of castles and churches.

There was also fierce competition within and between the Welsh-ruled lordships. Quarrels between sons over inheritance and between encroaching Welsh lords were endemic. Fragmentation was frequent, followed by valiant efforts at restoration. Thus Welsh rule in south-west Wales collapsed with the killing in 1093 of Rhys ap Tewdwr, and though considerably restored by the Lord Rhys, it fragmented again after the latter's death in 1197. Gwynedd Is Conwy grew and shrank frequently, often at the expense of Powys, a region whose gentler landscape and long eastern border often made it necessary to collaborate with England in order to survive.

Despite these bouts of savage internal competition, it is clear that as well as having their law, language and customs in common, constant pressure from outside strengthened a feeling of national identity among the Welsh. The name *Cymry* (fellow-countrymen) increasingly replaced 'Britons' as a standard form of self-identification. The English-derived *Wallia* and *Wallenses* became common in Welsh as well as English usage. Poets and chroniclers described princes as being 'the shield of Wales', 'prince of Wales' and even 'king of Wales', while English writers made derogatory generalisations about the national character of the Welsh. The idea of a national church based at St David's (ironically first mooted by a Norman bishop) gained favour. This national selfconsciousness reached its peak in Owain Glyndŵr's 'Pennal policy' of 1406, envisaging independence for the whole of Wales, with its own Church and universities.

By the early thirteenth century, Welsh resistance was largely concentrated in Gwynedd, the north-western realm, its strength fluctuating according to the ability of its leaders and the effectiveness of the opposition. Llywelyn the Great (d.1240) extended his rule over much of Wales, but his son Dafydd was forced to give up much of his patrimony in 1241 and died childless in 1246. Llywelyn's grandson, Llywelyn ap Gruffudd (Llywelyn II), then had to begin all over again, which he did with remarkable success. Great leader and warrior that he was, however, Llywelyn's rule could not stand up to the superior economic power of England once it was mobilised by a king of the calibre and ruthlessness of Edward I, whose armies included many Welshmen willing to take the king's penny. Llywelyn repeatedly refused to do homage to Edward, so the Welsh were crushed in 1277; Llywelyn was killed on 11 December 1282 and by the following June all resistance had ceased.

The building of Edward's mighty castles did not fully achieve their intimidatory purpose; there were fierce Welsh rebellions in 1287, 1294–95, 1314 and 1316, followed by the major revolt of Owain Glyndŵr in 1400. The last was much the most dangerous, since Owain was not simply protesting against the greed and maladministration of Crown officials; his revolt aimed at nothing less than Welsh independence. Nor was it simply the reaction of a single aggrieved and charismatic leader; it was the revolt of great numbers of the Welsh people

The massive tomb of Edward I in Westminster Abbey. Picture by Deiniol Morgan.

under their local leaders. Sieges of castles played a major part in the warfare; Owain's capture of Harlech and Aberystwyth gave him important administrative centres as well as prestige. But by 1412 serious resistance was over and Owain vanished. The next time a Welshman led a rebellion against the English Crown, it was not in the cause of Welsh independence but to take the Crown for himself, and it is well to remember that although Henry Tudor had been born and reared in Wales, only his paternal grandfather was Welsh.

The Castle Builders

It is easy to say glibly that Edward I built Caernarfon, or Gilbert de Clare, Caerphilly. What is actually meant is that they *willed* the construction of these castles for their own political and military purposes. Three parties were actually involved: the man who commissioned the castle, those who supervised the design and building, and the workmen. In the case of some of Edward's castles we have names for all three parties. But the Edwardian castles and Caerphilly are special cases. What actually happened in the case of nearly all the major Welsh castles is that they originated in obscurity and developed in complexity. Castles were founded, some were abandoned or destroyed, others altered, rebuilt or extended; they were besieged, captured and recaptured, and in many cases we cannot be sure of the dates of all these happenings.

The leaders who willed the castles into being and developed them, fall, as we have seen, into three categories: the English kings, the Marcher lords and the Welsh princes. Only a few castles other than the well-known Edwardian group can be called 'royal' creations. What is absolutely clear is that the vast majority of castles, from the humblest mottes to the mighty buildings at Kidwelly and Caerphilly, were the creations of the invading Normans and their successors, the Marcher lords and their lieutenants. Their history is complex, both because these men were involved in English, Irish and French affairs as well as Welsh, and because families frequently died out in the male line, passing the castles with heiresses into other families. Some individuals are easily confused thanks to their sharing baptismal names as well as ancestry. Thus a Richard (fitz Gilbert) de Clare ruled Ceredigion for twenty years before his death in 1136; a second Richard de Clare, nicknamed Strongbow (d.1176), made extensive conquests in Ireland; a third was lord of Glamorgan until he died in 1262. Five members of the Clare family were named Gilbert; the last died at Bannockburn in 1314, possessed of twelve castles in south-east Wales as well as some in England, and his lands were divided between his three sisters.

The castle builders included some remarkable leaders and strong characters. We know most about the individual kings: Henry I, the alarming; Henry II, the energetic and mercurial; John, sometimes able, sometimes virtually mad; the sometimes weak Henry III and the strongest of all, Edward I. Among the princes a number stand out: the enduring Gruffudd ap Cynan and his able son Owain Gwynedd; the charismatic Rhys ap Gruffudd; the powerful Llywelyn the Great and his grandson, Llywelyn II, whose men, according to an English chronicler, followed him as if glued to him. As for the Marcher lords, they had their own powerful dynasties, most notable de Braose, de Clare and Mortimer, as well as outstanding individuals like William Marshal, who rose from obscurity to be the greatest of royal ministers. A few women, too, could not be contained within the confines imposed to them: Gwenllian, who in 1136 led her husband's army against Kidwelly castle and died in battle; Joan, wife of Llywelyn the Great; Hawys Gadarn (the Strong) who defended Powis Castle in her husband's absence; Alice of Abergavenny, who according to the *Song of Dermot and the Earl*, was with the Norman-Welsh force which first invaded Ireland and personally beheaded seventy Irish prisoners after the battle of Baginbun in 1170, and King Dermot MacMurrough's daughter Aife, widow of Richard de Clare ('Strongbow').

Castles of the Welsh Princes

The phrase 'Welsh castle' is commonly used with two distinct meanings. Generally it means simply a castle in Wales, as opposed to an English castle (i.e. in England). It can also mean 'castle of a Welsh prince or lord'. This is a thorny subject indeed, as a few examples will show. Carreg Cennen is definitely a castle of Welsh *origin*, but the visible stonework is all post-1277. Cardigan is a castle of Norman *origin*, which

Cricieth's mighty gatehouse demonstrates the power of Llywelyn the Great.

was remade in stone by Rhys ap Gruffudd, though whether any of the remaining stonework dates from Rhys's time seems unlikely. Cricieth is a Welsh-built stone castle with Edwardian additions. Dolforwyn was Welsh-built, with no further changes. Even more complicated is Caergwrle, which was built by Llywelyn II's mercurial brother Dafydd when he was allied to Edward I, using English craftsmen and money. Many castles lack documentation; the attribution of some to Welsh initiative is a matter of judgement rather than certain fact. However, some ten per cent of all castles in Wales can reasonably claim Welsh origin. As early as 1111, the rash Powysian prince Cadwgan ap Bleddyn had intended to build a castle at Welshpool, but his violent death intervened. The first castle which can definitely be attributed to Welsh initiative is the motte near Cymer Abbey, Dolgellau, which the 'Welsh Chronicle' tells us was built in 1116 by the local prince Uchdryd ab Edwin, only to be destroyed a few months later. Building a castle implied a level of wealth and a sense of permanence to which not all Welsh leaders could aspire.

While the Welsh princes certainly had the resources to throw up mottes, it is just as difficult to attribute many of these to particular times or builders or national affinities as it is in the case of the stone castles. The best-known Welsh builders of castles were certainly Rhys ap Gruffudd (the Lord Rhys) in the twelfth century, and Llywelyn ab Iorwerth ('the Great') and Llywelyn ap Gruffudd in the thirteenth. But the rôle of Owain Gwynedd (d.1170) and his sons should not be underestimated, not to mention the rulers of Powys and the minor dynasts of east and south-east Wales.

What is typical of many of the castles we know to be of Welsh origin is their siting. The Normans may have chosen their early sites for strategic reasons, but they developed as centres of economic and administrative control. As already mentioned, the Welsh princes seem usually to have preferred the natural impregnability of crags and mountain sites; their courts or *llysoedd* on more level ground were their usual residences. From the primitive tower at Dinas Emrys and the mysterious ruins of Carndochan in the north, to the mighty crags of Carreg Cennen and Dinefwr in the south, the Welsh preference for siting their castles at altitude is clear.

The late Richard Avent wrote effectively on the Welsh princely castles in his bilingual *Castles of the Princes of Gwynedd* (1983) and in a number of Cadw guidebooks. The majority of Welsh castles have irregular plans dictated by their craggy sites, with little concern for enfilading fire along the walls against attackers. Towers were sometimes round, sometimes rectangular, sometimes in a typically Welsh D-shape (the apsidal tower). They were seen as independent strongpoints rather than as part of a fortified whole. Entrances were less complex than those of the great Anglo-Norman castles, though Dinefwr forced anyone attacking the gate to pass under fire along the wall, while Castell y Bere had fine rock-cut ditches with barbican and a drawbridge.

Paul R Davis's *Castles of the Welsh Princes* (Y Lolfa, 2007) discusses forty-three castles. He acknowledges the difficulties mentioned above in defining what is a 'Welsh castle' and rightly draws attention to the Welsh-built castles of Glamorgan and Gwent, but does not include the castles in Radnorshire which Paul Remfry has identified as possibly or probably Welsh in origin: Buddugre, Crug Eryr and Tomen Castle near Forest Inn. Indeed, it could even be argued that the great castle at Raglan was Welsh, though not princely, since William ap Thomas built the Yellow Tower of Gwent in the 1430s and 1440s and it was extended by the Herberts.

Despite all this, it seems clear that Welsh princes preferred their courts to their castles. Many of the surviving letters and other documents originated by Llywelyn ap Gruffudd are dated at places where there is no significant castle: Ystumanner, Pontymyneich, Berriew, Dinorben, Rhyd Gastell, Abereiddon, Sychdyn, Treuddyn, Dinas Teleri, Aberalwen. The list is extensive, the places often obscure to us. A Welsh prince relied primarily for protection on his environment, and at a personal level on his *teulu* (warband, literally the house-host; ironically, it now means 'family'), rather than on battlements.

Storm and Siege Warfare

Castles could be taken by surprise from without or treachery from within. Ladders, battering rams and mining techniques were used. The catapult and its variant the trebuchet could hurl stones at defensive walls; the ballista (a crossbow on a stand) fired bolts at the defenders. The walls could be directly attacked by teams of men protected by a 'tortoise' or roof on

Catapult missiles at Dolforwyn Castle.

wheels. Safer than a ladder but more costly was the belfrie or siege engine, a timber tower containing a ladder which offered protection to the men inside. Defenders replied with arrows, slings, crossbow-bolts and scalding fluids.

Although sometimes content, as described above, to destroy the settlements round a castle while not troubling to besiege it, the Welsh found it comparatively easy to storm the early earth and timber castles of the invaders, with surprise an important element. Castles sometimes rose and fell with remarkable rapidity. Thus the formidable Faulkes de Breauté built a castle at Aberystwyth (site uncertain) in 1211, but in the same year it was razed to the ground by the Welsh. The following year, so the *Chronicle of the Princes* tells us, Llywelyn the Great 'laid siege to all the castles which the king had built in Gwynedd [meaning north-west Wales] and took them all except two.' This is a powerful comment on the military weakness of so many castles.

Stone walls presented a sterner challenge which the light arms of guerilla troops could not easily overcome, though ingenuity sometimes prevailed. Ifor Bach of Senghenydd used ladders in his famous abduction of Earl Robert of Gloucester from Cardiff castle in 1158. In 1193, Maelgwn ap Rhys used slings and catapults to take Ystrad Meurig. In 1215 Llywelyn the Great led an alliance of Welsh lords against the castles of the south, capturing no fewer than nine, but all his siege engines failed to take Builth in 1231. The Welsh used undermining at Degannwy in 1250–52. Cunning, treachery and military strength also brought Welsh successes against castles at Tenby (1153), Tafolwern (1162), Wizo's Castle (1193), Cilgerran (1199), Dinefwr (1213) and Builth (1260), to name only some. In the mid-thirteenth century, Llywelyn ap Gruffudd was well able to take castles by storm, as were Owain Glyndŵr and his allies in the fifteenth century. Although castles were still resisting siege in the Civil Wars of the seventeenth century, their eventual doom had already become clear when Aberystwyth was attacked by cannon in 1408. Stone walls were powerless against gunpowder.

Afterlife

Between rebellions and after Glyndŵr's failure, castle garrisons were tiny and the condition of the buildings largely one of decay, though during the Wars of the Roses a number of castles were part of the action, especially Harlech, the last Lancastrian castle in the kingdom to surrender. They played their last military rôle during the Civil Wars. Wales was largely royalist, and a large number of castles were held for Charles I by his loyal supporters and had to be reduced by parliamentarian siege. By this time, cannon were far more effective than they had been in previous sieges; one by one the castles fell, and some were ordered by Cromwell to be reduced to rubble; again Harlech was the last, though fortunately it was simply too strong to wreck.

Carew Castle, showing its range of Elizabethan windows.

With the coming of peace after 1485, the richest Welsh squires found uses for a few stone castles. Henry Tudor's chief Welsh supporter, Sir Rhys ap Thomas, created domestic accommodation within several of his Welsh castles, while Sir John Perrot made splendid additions to Carew and Laugharne, though they have long since become ruins. Powis Castle remained a lordly home well into the twentieth century. Other castles were adapted in more recent times; eighteenth-century improvements did much for Picton, Powis and Chirk as stately homes, while nineteenth-century extravagance saw Cardiff and Castell Coch become fantasies in stone. Other Victorian castles were created largely or entirely from scratch to reflect the egos of their creators: Gwrych, Bodelwyddan, Cyfarthfa, Glandyfi and Penrhyn.

Even if we disregard the mottes and ringworks which form the majority of castles in Wales, the remote or difficult siting of most stone castles made their adaptation for domestic use difficult. A few, as we have seen, were deliberately destroyed, especially in 1646–47. Others were pillaged for building stone and other materials. These depredations can easily be recognised, for example at Rhuddlan, because the walls appear to have been gnawed by giant beavers; the good surfacing stone has been taken, while the rubble remains. Builth's stone vanished entirely. Some (Dinefwr is an example) were cherished as eye-catchers in the picturesque landscape. Some are now in municipal ownership, others on private sites, while many of the finest are owned by the government and cared for by Cadw, the Welsh equivalent of English Heritage. A number of castles have been excavated by archaeologists. A good deal of this work has been to make castle buildings more attractive and accessible to visitors; there is much to be done in studying the landscape archaeology of castles in Wales.

Castles in Art and Poetry

A few Welsh castles were depicted by seventeenth-century artists, including Francis Place and Thomas Dineley. In the eighteenth century, both landscape and the medieval past began to interest people. This developing taste was exploited by Samuel and Nathaniel Buck, who between 1728 and 1753 recorded hundreds of historic buildings, many of them in Wales. Their work is rather awkward and stilted, but fascinating to students because the ruins were more complete then than they are now. With the development of Romantic art in the second half of the eighteenth century, Welsh castles became a popular subject, part of the huge development of landscape painting across Europe. A number of them were painted in all their splendour by the great Welsh artist Richard Wilson (1713–82), who clearly saw in them an iconography of the Welsh past, especially in his painting of Dinas Brân. Several

An 18th-century print of Richard Wilson's Pembroke Castle.
National Library of Wales.

41

of these pictures were bought by aristocratic Welsh patrons, caught up in the revival of interest in medieval Welsh culture and history at the time, a revival of which these pictures were a part.

The English and foreign artists who began to flock to Wales saw castles as a vital part of the picturesque landscape. As well as Wilson, Paul Sandby and Julius Caesar Ibbetson, these included John Sell Cotman, the David Coxes (father and son), Thomas Girtin, John Varley and especially JMW Turner; all artists gave the Welsh castle iconic form. Turner painted at least seventeen Welsh castles after his tours of the country, often with more imagination than antiquarian accuracy, and he knew Thomas Pennant's *The Journey to Snowdon*, which helped him understand something of Welsh history. By contrast, contemporary Welsh artists have shown little interest in castles, whether as a focus of landscape or symbol of Welsh nationality, except when commissioned to do so. Interested readers should track down Paul Joyner's *Dolbadarn: Studies on a Theme* (Aberystwyth, 1990). Peter Humphries's *On the Trail of Turner in North and South Wales* (Cadw) is also good value.

The same Romantic-Gothic movement saw poets looking at castle ruins and finding inspiration in them. The first to do so was a Welshman, John Dyer, whose 1728 poem on the Tywi valley embraces the castles at Dinefwr and Dryslwyn:

Old castles on the cliffs arise,
Proudly towering in the skies!
Rushing from the woods, the spires
Seem from hence ascending fires!...
While, ever and anon, there falls
Huge heap of hoary moulder'd walls...

In later generations the Welsh poets Twm o'r Nant and Taliesin o Eifion, as well as Wordsworth himself, were similarly inspired, at Cricieth, Dinas Brân and Conwy respectively, to muse on the transience of earthly glory.

Authorities

A list of authorities other than those already cited, including websites, is provided with Appendix A. Alas, even the best and most scholarly authorities cannot solve every problem. Medieval dating is beset with difficulties; medieval architecture and archaeology have their difficulties, as do medieval history and politics. In the desire to provide the reader with a narrative, it is easy to slip unintentionally from speculation to assertion, from assertion to supposed fact and thence a dubious certainty.

The historical background can be studied at several levels. J Graham Jones's *A History of Wales* in the University of Wales Press's pocket series is invaluable, as is John Davies's *A History of Wales* (Penguin, second edition, 2007). For the detailed military history Sir John Edward Lloyd's *A History of Wales* (Longman, third edition,1939) and JE Morris's *The Welsh Wars of Edward I* (Sutton, 1998, reprint) are still fundamental. So is Sir Rees Davies's *The Age of Conquest* (Oxford, several reprints) and his equally authoritative *The Revolt of Owain Glyn Dŵr* (Oxford, 1995). David Moore's *The Welsh Wars of Independence* (Tempus, 2005) is valuable especially for chapters 9 and 10. Ian Soulsby's *The Towns of Medieval Wales* (Chichester, 1983) is useful for relating some castles to their boroughs. Sean Davies's *Welsh Military Institutions* (Cardiff, 2004) has many insights. Cadw's guidebooks by Richard Avent, Jeremy Knight, Lawrence Butler, Arnold Taylor and others are of the highest standard. The only pocket-sized guides available are those published by Mike Salter's Folly Press.

THE CASTLES...

The Thirteen Historic Counties of Wales

ANGLESEY

BEAUMARIS

SH 607 763. Cadw. Fee.

• **Access** This last of Edward I's great castles, the acme of military planning of the age, is easily found at the east end of the delightful town of Beaumaris, itself well worth a visit, particularly the fine parish church and the historic gaol. There is a large car park on the promenade. Dramatic productions and historical reconstructions figure at some summer weekends, and there is a permanent exhibition.

• **History** Prior to the invasion and conquest of 1283, Anglesey had hardly been subjected to any Norman presence, though a motte survives at Aberlleiniog from a brief incursion in the late eleventh century. In 1294 Madog ap Llywelyn's rebels had seized and held the unfinished castle at Caernarfon, thus effectively controlling the Menai Straits. For Edward to build at Beaumaris would at once give control of the Menai Straits and the island itself. Work therefore began, not without difficulty, on the 'Fair Fen' (French *Beau marais*) after the rebellion was quelled, hung fire during the war with Scotland (1300–06) and then continued until 1330, but the task was never completed. At least £25,000 was spent in the process.

Despite its complex defences, Glyndŵr's supporters captured and held the castle for two years (1403–05), while the luckless English burgesses in the undefended town suffered. Eventually town walls were provided when no longer needed, but have since vanished. The much-admired Catholic priest-martyr William Davies was long imprisoned in the castle before his execution in 1593. During the Civil Wars, the newly ennobled viscount Thomas Bulkeley of the great local family held the castle for the king until surrendering in 1646. In 1648 royalist insurgents led by Thomas's son Richard seized the castle briefly, but it was again surrendered, and passes out of history.

• **Buildings**   The castle and borough were built on a virgin site, while the nearby Welsh borough of Llan-faes was moved to Rhosyr (Newborough) to avoid competition; stone from the houses was used to supplement the locally quarried grit and limestone. Swans on the moat delight visitors, but unlike Conwy, Harlech and Caernarfon, so impressive without, low-lying Beaumaris is more impressive within its massive and perfectly symmetrical walls and towers. It's hardly surprising that rugged Wales has few moats around its castles, but sea-level Beaumaris was easily surrounded, and much of the moat remains, though part has been filled in. The octagonal outer curtain wall is pierced by two gates, deliberately placed out of line with the great gatehouses to frustrate attackers. Next to the south gateway are the remains of the sea-gate and its dock, which allowed the provisioning of the castle directly from the sea. As at Harlech, the outer ward is simply a narrow space between the lower outer and much higher inner

Beaumaris walls and moat.

curtain walls, giving defenders on both levels a clear field of fire. The inner wall is over four metres thick and has sixteen towers, still rich in passages and stairs. The inner fortress has six towers apart from the gatehouses.

The intended grandeur of the defences is lessened by the fact that all the main towers were left unfinished at two storeys high instead of the intended three; only the outer front of the north gatehouse reaches the intended height. Indeed the south gatehouse may never have been occupied, but the main apartments in the north gatehouse, intended as royal accommodation, were usable. Certainly it is clear that there was to be separate accommodation for eleven households. There are traces of foundation walls within the extensive inner ward, but what they were (kitchen? stables? both?) is not known. The finest remaining stonework in any Welsh castle of the period is to be found in the lovely chapel in the eastern middle tower; look for the five lancet windows and trefoil arcading below.

BRECONSHIRE

BRECON

SO 044 286. Hotel-owned.

• **Access and Buildings** Little is publicly visible of this once important castle. In the Castle Hotel garden you can see the great hall with its fine lancet windows, while the Ely tower and motte stand in the private gardens of the bishop of Swansea and Brecon. To reach the hotel from the town bridge over the Usk, turn west into the Avenue, bearing right up the hill and then sharp right into Castle Square and the hotel car park. Permission to visit the garden is readily given at the hotel

Brecon castle hall.

desk. The cathedral further up the hill deserves a visit.

• **History** The Normans had occupied this strategic point above the Usk by 1093, building a castle and founding the town, with a Benedictine priory. For a century alien rule was largely undisturbed until Llywelyn the Great attacked it in 1217, 1231 and 1233, inflicting damage on the town but failing to seize the castle, a feat finally accomplished by Llywelyn ap Gruffudd in 1262. His control of the lordship of Brycheiniog fizzled out with the war of 1276–77. Welsh rebels failed to capture it in 1282 and 1294; even Owain Glyndŵr's supporters failed. Edward II succeeded in taking it in 1322; its last siege was in 1645, when the parliamentarian army drove out the royalist garrison and slighted the buildings.

BRONLLYS

SO 149 346. Cadw. Open access.

• **Access** The village of Bronllys is on the A438 from Brecon to Hereford. The castle is half a mile to the south-east on the Bronllys–Talgarth A479 which, further south, crosses a fine scenic pass to join the Brecon–Abergavenny road near Tretower. High hedges and trees conceal the castle tower. There is no car park, but the road is wide enough to park safely.

Bronllys Keep.

• **History** The site was apparently chosen to guard the local roads, and stands above the confluence of the rivers Llynfi and Dulais. The large motte was built around the turn of the twelfth century, either by Richard fitz Pons, a follower of Bernard de Neufmarché the conqueror of this area, or Richard's son Walter, who took the surname Clifford from his father's English lordship. It remained a timber castle until the time of Richard's great-grandson Walter Clifford III; he added the massive red sandstone keep after he inherited the lordship of Bronllys in 1221. Clifford's wife was Margaret, daughter of Llywelyn the Great. It was briefly seized by the government of Henry III in 1233 in the frequent baronial wars, and was the scene of negotations between the Crown and Llywelyn. Intriguingly, with the end of the Clifford dynasty the castle was taken in 1311 by a Welshman, Rhys ap Hywel, as a reward for his loyalty to the Mortimers and Bohuns, but in 1351 it was lost to the Bohuns. It became a ruin and played no part in the Glyndŵr rebellion or the Civil Wars.

• **Buildings** The site gives an initially claustrophobic feeling, partly on account of the trees, partly because only the motte and tower are open to visitors; the extensive inner and outer baileys are on private land. The steep climb to the doorway gives good views from the entrance. Inside, stairs on one side go down to the basement (with a ten-foot drop from the bottom stair); on the other side stairs go up from the hall to the second and third floors – the latter a fourteenth-century addition. These provided the castle's domestic accommodation.

BUILTH

SO 044 510. Open access.

• **Access and Site** Builth seems ashamed of its castle. There are no signs to help motorists and few for pedestrians. Park in the Strand riverside car park (well signposted, with tourist office, but if approaching on the A470 from the north or south-east one has to follow the one-way system through the town to reach it). Walk from the Strand to the T-junction where the A470 comes from the Wye bridge and turns left, but turn right into Broad Street. Next to the Lion pub is an unnamed passageway at the end of which there is a slate sign pointing left towards the castle. There is a descriptive plaque by the gate. Alternatively, Castle Street is accessible from the A470 near the Arts Centre; there is room to park and a stile in the hedge on the right with a very small sign. The site itself is an

Builth from the air. Crown copyright RCAHMW.

awesome tumble of massive earthworks, seriously overgrown with thistles and scrub, once crowned by a major Edwardian castle, on which £1,666 was spent between 1277 and 1294.

• **History** The huge motte, marking the northern extent of the Braose lordship of Brecon, of which the Welsh *cantref* of Buellt/Builth formed part, was built by William de Braose or his son Philip before 1100 to guard the Wye crossing. Destroyed by Rhys ap Gruffudd in 1168 but rebuilt by William de Braose II, in 1208 the castle was confiscated by King John and re-fortified by him, but the defiant de Braose brothers Giles and Reginald seized the castle again in 1215. In 1223 it resisted attack by Llywelyn the Great. When Llywelyn captured William de Braose III in 1228, he secured a ransom of £2,000 and Builth Castle, as well as an agreement for his son Dafydd to marry William's daughter Isabel. But then Llywelyn caught William committing adultery with his wife Siwan; in his wrath he hanged William, while securing that the marriage went ahead, such was the *realpolitik* of the time. Isabel was excluded from the division of her father's lands among the daughters, and in 1241 Builth passed with an heiress to Roger Mortimer, the dominant Marcher lord of the day, who began to refortify it in stone.

In 1260 Llywelyn ap Gruffudd seized the lordship and took the castle, apparently by treachery within; it was then utterly demolished by his south Welsh allies. Llywelyn lost control of the lordship in 1277 when Edward I's general, the Earl of Lincoln, took it back. Edward's men were soon building a new and larger castle incorporating the motte, baileys and ditching already in place; Edward's constable was a Welshman, Hywel ap Meurig, a major ally of Roger Mortimer and the king. In 1282 Llywelyn failed to recapture Builth on his last desperate expedition to mid-Wales, and was killed near Cilmeri, two miles west of Builth on the A483. Near Cilmeri can be seen the striking monument to Llywelyn's memory and the well where his severed head is said to have been washed. For centuries local people were known as *Bradwyr Buellt* (the traitors of Builth) for their supposed part in the episode, which is commemorated in Builth by a large wallpainting on the building overlooking the A470 T-junction by the bridge. The castle was defended successfully against the rebellion of Madog ap Llywelyn in 1294, when it was blockaded for six weeks, and garrisoned against Owain Glyndŵr's revolt in 1401. In 1691 the town burnt down, and any remaining stonework was entirely used in rebuilding.

CRICKHOWELL

SO 218 183. Open access.

• **Access** This shattered ruin, one of a chain of castles in the Usk valley, stands on the south-eastern edge of the little town, close to the A40 from Abergavenny to Brecon. It is marked on the OS map as Alisby's Castle, and is an open recreational area. It is best reached from Abergavenny by turning left off the A40 into Castle Road; from Brecon, drive through the town past the park on the right and turn sharp right into Castle Road.

• **History and Site** The twelfth-century motte and timber castle were probably the work of the Turberville family, while the stonework was done by the husband of the Turberville heiress, the wonderfully named Sir Grimbald Pauncefoot, from 1272, who was one of Edward I's household knights. The castle passed into Mortimer hands but in 1402 was restored to Sir Grimbald's great-grandson Sir John, who refortified the castle. The site passed via Crown ownership to Sir William Herbert of Raglan, and much of the castle's original fabric was probably robbed by house-builders in the town. The motte is still massive despite erosion by feet and weather. Of the

Crickhowell motte.

extensive red sandstone walls and castle fabric only two large fragments remain, a double tower close to the motte, and the gatehouse, originally having two towers, one of which has been reduced almost to ground level. Despite this destruction, the fragments impress by their height, and between them it is just possible to envision a powerful castle which, apart from its brief garrisoning against Owain Glyndŵr in 1403, played little known part in history.

HAY-ON-WYE

SO 229 423. Private.

• **Access**   I have only included this sadly wrecked castle because Hay is such a busy tourist centre and the ruin dominates the centre of the town. The Castle Bookshop is based at the far end of later additions to the medieval ruin, but the ancient part is closed to the public.

• **History and Buildings** The original castle was a motte near the parish church; the first stone castle was probably the work of the infamous William de Braose (see Abergavenny castle, p.168) before 1200; it was captured by King John in 1207 and William's wife Maud taken into captivity and starved to death. John burnt town and castle in 1216 while putting down a de Braose rebellion. The castle cannot have been in the best condition when Llywelyn the Great stormed it successfully in 1231 as part of his great sweep through eastern Wales. During Simon de Montfort's rebellion against Henry III, Hay was captured in 1264 by Prince Edward and again in 1265 by de Montfort. Glyndŵr's rebels may have inflicted some damage on town and castle, but it held out, and remained the home of the Dukes of Buckingham until the last duke was executed in 1521. The medieval castle was abandoned in favour of a large house with Dutch gables added in the seventeenth century. Hay's thirteenth-century town walls have almost entirely disappeared.

The sad wreckage of Hay castle.

TRETOWER

SO 185 213. Cadw. Fee.

• **Access** This site is fascinating not so much for its castle as for the unique medieval manor-house close by. Since access to the castle is only through the house, castle enthusiasts might as well enjoy the latter in addition. Visitors should also notice the splendid farm building opposite the entrance, although it is not open to the public at the time of writing. Lying as Tretower does close to the junction of the A479 from Talgarth with the A40 between Brecon and Abergavenny, access is easy and parking available. The official guidebook covers both castle and manor; the present overview is restricted to the castle. The approach from house to castle passes through two meadows, one of which is often grazed by rare White Park cattle.

• **History** The importance of the routeway junction where the river Rhiangoll flows into the Usk, and the fertile ground there, was long recognised; there is a standing stone and a Roman fort nearby. With the Norman occupation of the Usk valley by the turn of the twelfth century, one Picard, a follower of Bernard de Neufmarché, built the motte. It was fortified by his son with a stone shell-keep and a bailey with walls and towers. The castle is not known to have been attacked by the Welsh, but Llywelyn ap Gruffudd gained the lordship of Brecon (smaller in size than the later county) in 1262, and Roger Picard, like other local leaders, found it advisable to acknowledge Llywelyn's overlordship. By this time a massive tower had been built inside the original keep.

With the passing of Welsh independence the need for such a fortification had gone, and the Picards had begun the creation of the manor-house by the turn of the fourteenth century. Through the marriage of the Picard heiress with Ralph Bluet

Tretower's concentric keep.

of Raglan, Tretower came by purchase to Sir William ap Thomas of Raglan. His son Sir William Herbert gave it to his Yorkist follower Roger Vaughan, who restored and extended the manor-house. Both men were executed after Lancastrian victories, but the Vaughan family retained the castle and house until both were sold in 1783 and the house became a farm. The poet Henry Vaughan was a member of the family who would have known the house well, but he seems to have lived mainly at Scethrog, between Bwlch and Brecon. Eventually Tretower was bought by the Brecknock Society and transferred to the Ministry of Works in 1930.

• **Buildings** The thirteenth-century bailey wall is on the right of the approach path, and beyond it are large corrugated-iron farm buildings where once stood the medieval hall, stable and other structures. The massive red sandstone keep, in appearance a tower within a tower, is the most impressive feature. Its entrance is reached by walking round the further side to the ruined gatehouse. The original shell-keep had buildings (hall, solar and kitchen) within it at first-floor level which largely disappeared with the thirteenth-century creation of the inner tower, but some fine early architectural details survive, including small romanesque windows easily missed by those who are more intrigued by the giant vertical cracks in the outer wall. The outline high on the north-west side indicates the former roof over an access passage-bridge from the inner tower to the outer wall. Below it are horizontal lines of holes where a later, undated building was added to the tower. The walls of the great inner tower are nine feet thick. The tower was roofed, and each floor-level formed a single chamber.

CAERNARFONSHIRE

CAERNARFON

SH 477 627. Cadw. Fee.

• **Access** The palpable Welshness of Caernarfon today would mortify the town's creator. Edward I planted his castle and walled English borough to intimidate and exclude the Welsh save as day visitors; now the Welsh are the residents and the English the visitors. Access to the castle needs no description except to reassure first-time visitors that for most of the year the large quayside car park beneath the castle walls has room for all. The Royal Welsh Fusiliers museum is housed in the Queen's tower. There are historical re-enactments and other performances on some summer weekends. Although there is currently no access to the town walls, they deserve viewing.

• **History** Caernarfon is a special place. Roman Segontium can be visited on the hill above the town, on the A4086 to Llanberis; Hen Waliau ('old walls') is another Roman site lying on the A487 south of its junction with the A4085 Waunfawr/ Beddgelert road. The medieval Welsh tale 'The Dream of Macsen' celebrates the splendour of Caer Seiont (an alternative name for the early settlement), its princess Elen and the emperor of Rome's passion for her. The *Historia Brittonum* of the tenth-century records the tomb of Constantine the Great as being at Caernarfon, and a body, supposedly that of 'Maxen' (i.e. Magnus Maximus, emperor of Gaul, d.AD 388) was found in Caernarfon in 1283 during the building of the present castle. Edward would certainly have been aware of the site's symbolism.

Hugh, Earl of Chester, had swept through north Wales in 1088 and built a motte and bailey here, only for the Welsh to

Caernarfon from the Menai Straits.

reoccupy the site in 1115. The motte was contained within the east end of the new castle which Edward's men began to build in 1283 with extraordinary speed. The intention was to provide a base for royal visits and a major governmental centre. Edward's royal ambitions for the castle were manifest in 1284 when Queen Eleanor, who had been provided with a lawn, gave birth among the building works to her fourteenth child, Edward, who was later presented to the Welsh as their new prince, thus appropriating to him the title first acknowledged by the Crown for Llywelyn ap Gruffudd in 1267. The infant became heir to the throne after his only surviving brother Alfonso died later in 1284, and he was later crowned as Edward II. The splendid town walls were completed in two years, and the long river-wall and east end of the castle were finished by 1289. There was then a lull; the expense could not be sustained, and the Welsh appeared to have been pacified.

Then the revolt of Madog ap Llywelyn in 1294 brought destruction to the town and serious damage to the half-finished castle before work was eventually resumed, to continue through the reign of Edward II. By 1330 at least £25,000 had been spent, a truly gigantic sum, but the original impetus was ebbing and the work never completed. Thanks to seaborne supplies the castle was easily able to withstand the Glyndŵr rebellion despite the attacks of his French allies, even though the hinterland was in rebel hands and the castle isolated for several years. It was again defended stubbornly during the Civil Wars, changing hands several times before finally surrendering in June 1646.

Parts of the castle continued to be used into the nineteenth century. A local businessman and deputy constable of the castle, Sir Llewelyn Turner (1823–1903), employed an architect to refurbish the battlements, roof and stairs. The improvements made it possible for Lloyd George to stage the proclamation of Edward VII's son as Prince of Wales in 1911, and for the similar ceremony for Prince Charles in 1969 in a government effort to channel the contemporary revival of Welsh national feeling.

• **Buildings** Caernarfon is more familiar from photographs and paintings than any other Welsh castle, yet its massive presence is still overwhelming, especially when viewed from the quay, where the banded limestone and polygonal towers, seemingly in imitation of the iconic fifth-century walls of Constantinople (see p.9), can best be seen. Like that city, the castle has its own Golden Gate, Porth yr Aur, at the west end. The Constantinian inheritance is mentioned in the medieval Welsh biography of Gruffudd ap Cynan, where Caernarfon is described as Constantine's city. Nowhere else in this island, despite the competition from Conwy, Beaumaris and Harlech, is the rampant imperial ego of Edward I, burnished with trappings of chivalry, so apparent. One is irresistibly reminded of vast modern expenditure on armaments, not as serious protection but as imperial self-promotion beyond all military needs.

The shape of both castle and town was determined by the site, which is a small peninsula between the rivers Seiont and Cadnant. A ditch was dug around the castle itself as well as round the town, and the main access was and is through the King's Gate on the northern side. Here the visitor between the eastern or upper ward and the western lower ward, with the Chamberlain tower opposite. Clockwise from the King's Gate are the Granary, North-east and Watch towers, the Queen's gate, the Cistern, Black, Chamberlain, Queen's, Eagle and Well towers. Each tower is different; most impressive is the Eagle tower, so called for the (much eroded) Roman eagle figures crowning its 128-foot summit. The higher level of the upper ward is the result of levelling the motte in 1870.

The first phase of building (1283–92) was directed by Master James of St George, and includes all the towers from the North-east to the Eagle tower; the emphasis is on the deterrent, imperial function of the castle. The second phase (1296–1323), supervised by Walter of Hereford, shows a certain relaxation in favour of improved accommodation. The impressive stone banding of the south wall was abandoned in favour of plainer masonry, and the north wall is rather thinner, while several traceried windows can be seen high up in royal apartments. Outside in a niche above the gate is a 1321 figure of Edward II, who having been born here was known as Edward of Caernarfon. The freestone in windows and doors is gritstone from Moel-y-don.

The variety of structures within the castle is impressive, even though some, particularly the King's Gate with its five doors and six portcullises, were never completed, and the great hall is now only marked by its foundations in the lower ward. The Queen's Gate at the east end, now totally inaccessible from outside, was once reached by a great ramp. These two entrances were clearly designed, in different ways, to make an indelible impact on those admitted. There were several private chapels as well as a main chapel in the King's Gate. The walls are honeycombed with passages and stairs largely accessible to the visitor and delighted in by children.

CONWY

SH 783774/SH 78367744. Cadw. Fee.

• **Access** Conwy Castle and town deserve a whole day. Conwy railway station (request stop) is on the line from Chester to Holyhead, below the castle. By car from the A55 follow signs through a series of roundabouts along the A547 towards the mighty borough walls. Immediately after passing through the wall turn left and follow signs to the long-term car park, which gives easy walking access; the short-term car park is so busy in summer as not to be worth trying. When you've seen the castle you have the choice of a pleasant waterfront with summer boats plying the river, walking sections of the magnificent walls and visiting the fourteenth-century Aberconwy House (National Trust) and the 1576 Plas Mawr (Cadw), close to each other.

• **History** Before the Edwardian conquest this site was the home of the Cistercian abbey of Aberconwy, originally founded elsewhere in 1186 but moved here by Llywelyn the Great in about 1200. He and his two sons were both buried in the church which, vastly altered, still serves the town, while Edward I had the abbey moved up the Conwy valley to Maenan. The main Welsh centre of rule in the area was at **Deganwy** (SH 781

794) whose hummocky site east of the Conwy is clearly visible from the castle, though little masonry survives and the site is really only worth visiting for the view, and to evoke distant memories of the sixth-century king Maelgwn Gwynedd.

Even after Llywelyn's death at Builth on 11 December 1282, Edward I's campaign of conquest still had months to run. Advancing from Rhuddlan, his army moved up the Conwy valley to capture Dolwyddelan and then back northwards to Aberconwy. The site offered a strong position on the estuary where it could be provisioned by sea if besieged. It was probably intended as the main centre for administering his new principality of north Wales, hence the size and strength of the building work, but administration was eventually centred at Caernarfon.

Castle and borough developed as one under the supervision

Conwy, looking w. from the e. tower over the main ward.

of Master James of St George and master craftsmen from England and France, and the main building works were in place by 1287, an astonishing feat considering the amount of stone involved. It was just as well for Edward, since when he returned to Wales in the winter of 1294–95 to put down the rebellion of Madog ap Llywelyn he found himself blockaded in Conwy for several weeks before the Welsh were defeated by Edward's generals and their crossbow-men.

Before long the castle's timbers started rotting and there are frequent references to leaking roofs. Major reconstruction work installed lead on the roofs, with fifteen massive arches supporting the weight. The story of the capture of the castle by Owain Glyndŵr's kinsmen, the Tudor brothers Rhys and Gwilym, is remarkable. Early in 1401 they were marked men, having supported Glyndŵr's initial rising; on Good Friday they seized the castle while the garrison was at prayer and held it for two months before handing it back to the Crown and gaining pardon for themselves, at the price of handing over some of their followers for execution.

The castle continued to decay into the seventeenth century, but in 1644 it was put into military order at his own expense by John Williams, a Conwy man who was archbishop of York and a strong royalist. Disgusted however by the king's lack of support and alarmed by the parliamentarian threat to his beloved home town, the archbishop surrendered the castle in 1645. The parliamentarian occupiers tied the Irish prisoners held in the castle back-to-back and threw them into the sea. In 1655 it was ordered to be slighted and severe damage was inflicted on the Bakehouse Tower. It became a spectacular ruin, inspiring one of JMW Turner's finest castle paintings. Meanwhile the town never really outgrew its walls and remains the finest British example of a medieval *bastide* or fortified borough.

Telford's suspension bridge of 1826 and the tubular railway bridge of 1848, both linking Chester with Bangor and Holyhead, brought more visitors to Conwy to admire the ruined castle and walls, and efforts began to make them accessible. Responsibility for the castle passed to Conwy Council in 1885, and to the Ministry of Works in 1953. In 1987, with its walls, it became a World Heritage site.

• **Buildings** The castle is at once integral to the town, all of a piece with the walls in material and design, and yet apart from it. Entry to the castle from within the town was made difficult; a drawbridge crossed a ditch to a defended entrance by the north-west tower (where the modern path now leads). The castle itself is divided into two wards; the eastern ward and buildings formed the king's own accommodation, and could be reached from the western ward only through a cross-wall with gate and drawbridge. It did however have access by a water-gate from the river, so that water-borne royalty and privileged visitors did not have to enter the town and then the western ward to gain entry.

One way of appreciating the castle is to make for the King's Tower at the far end from the entrance. Walk through the west ward, past the 91-foot deep well to the south-east corner and climb. The views are spectacular. East of you are the three Conwy bridges and below, the east barbican. To the west in the middle distance the south wall of the town rises to its highest peak; don't miss visiting it. Below lie the east and west wards. Ranked on the north and south are the eight great towers, and immediately below you the royal apartments. The four royal towers are crowned with turrets. The north-east tower held the chapel, where there is now a display on the subject of castle chapels.

In the royal ward there is a complex of rooms, all at first-floor level, including the king's great chamber to the east, the presence chamber and privy chamber to the south, with a parlour or servants' hall below. In the west ward, the buildings on the south side are (from east to west) the main chapel, the great hall and lesser hall, with the prison tower leading off midway. On the north side are the kitchen foundations. The two fine arches are the survivors of those built to support the leaded roofs. All·the masonry is of local volcanic stone.

CRICIETH

SH 500 377. Cadw. Fee.

• **Access** A short walk brings you from the railway station to the fine castle, perched on the sea's edge in this attractive little town, or it is easily reached by car from Porthmadog (A497) or Caernarfon (A487:B4411). Car parking is limited. In June enjoy the flowers on the rocks outside the castle walls, especially wild thyme.

• **History** Clearly the work of Llywelyn the Great, Cricieth castle was, in 1239, the prison of Llywelyn's son Gruffudd, incarcerated there by his half-brother Dafydd, heir to Llywelyn when their father was terminally ill. Twenty years later it was again a prison, this time for Maredudd ap Rhys, a south Wales prince who had turned against Llywelyn ap Gruffudd. It was captured by Edward I's army in March 1283; the next year Edward constituted Cricieth a borough. Later he used the castle to hold Scottish prisoners of war. In 1295 Cricieth's English garrison, under siege in the rebellion of Madog ap Llywelyn, was relieved by sea. In the mid-fourteenth century the constable was Sir Hywel ap Gruffudd, better known as Hywel y Fwyall (the Axe) thanks to his skill with that weapon in Edward III's French wars. The axe had a place laid at the family table for generations. Iolo Goch gives a fine description of the veteran warrior, with his wife and her maidens

Cricieth. Photograph: Paul Davis.

sewing silk by the light of a glazed window. The castle was garrisoned against Glyndŵr in 1401 but stormed by him and thenceforward falls out of history, eventually to be given to the state in 1933 by its then owner, Lord Harlech.

• **Buildings** Why did Llywelyn the Great build Cricieth at all? The area was safely within Gwynedd's boundaries, far from external threat and with no known internal danger. It was surely part of his programme of strengthening his position as a medieval sovereign, a demonstration of his power as much as a necessary defence. The splendid gatehouse, admittedly reinforced after it was lost to Edward I in 1283, shows Llywelyn's willingness to learn from English examplars. The model was probably Beeston in Cheshire, built by Ranulf, earl of Chester, Llywelyn's ally and friend. An earlier generation of historians had believed that the present masonry was mostly English work, but it is now accepted that Llywelyn built the gatehouse and inner curtain ward, Llywelyn ap Gruffudd the outer walls, and Edward I or II the north 'Engine' tower as well as improving the outer walls. The masonry is of local origin, with Anglesey grit supplying the dressing stone. A tiny crucified Christ made of copper and enamel (possibly from Limoges) now in the National Museum of Wales at Cardiff was discovered in the gatehouse, suggesting that it contained a chapel of which no traces remain.

DOLBADARN

SH 586 598. Cadw. Fee.

• **Access** Although the environs of Dolbadarn castle have been drastically altered by the huge Electric Mountain power scheme, this Welsh castle still dominates lake Padarn when approached from the west, and itself is dwarfed by the great Snowdon massif. Unsurprisingly it captivated generations of visiting romantic artists. From the west, the A4086 bypasses Llanberis village close to Lake Padarn and runs towards the castle; from the east the road runs through a splendid glaciated landscape past Lake Peris. The castle is situated by an awkward bend in the road where parking is hardly possible; cars should be left at the public car park between the lakes. Cadw's excellent guidebook combines this site with Dolwyddelan and Castell y Bere.

• **History** Dolbadarn is poorly documented. It was probably built by Llywelyn the Great (d.1240). His grandson Llywelyn ap Gruffudd, recreated and extended this dominance, but at a price. When Llywelyn was opposed by his elder brother Owain in 1255, he imprisoned Owain for more than twenty years, and according to tradition this was the place of captivity. The bound figure of the prince can be seen in Turner's famous painting of the castle. Owain was released in 1277 after Llywelyn's first defeat by Edward and given land in Llŷn.

Dolbadarn Keep. Photograph: Paul Davis.

After the death of Llywelyn at Cilmeri in December 1282, his brother Dafydd continued the hopeless struggle against Edward. He issued his last documents from this castle, claiming the now empty title 'Prince of Wales and Lord of Snowdon'. In June 1283 he was captured here and taken away to be hanged, drawn and quartered at Shrewsbury on 2 October. Edward retained Dolbadarn as a royal manor, and repairs were carried out in 1303–4, but the castle played no further part in history other than as centre of the most dramatic of Welsh landscapes.

• **Buildings** The castle's site is intriguing. It obviously gives absolute control over the Llanberis pass, but the other two passes through Snowdonia, Nant Gwynant and Rhyd-ddu, do not have castles. However, Dolbadarn's central position suggests that when danger threatened there would have been sentries in the other passes who could report back and necessary action could be taken. In fact no English army penetrated the fastnesses of Snowdonia between 1100 and 1282.

The visitor passed through the drystone curtain wall to view the fine round tower-keep, built largely of well-mortared slate, demonstrating that Llywelyn well knew the Marcher fashions of castle building, perhaps himself employing English masons. It had ampler accommodation than most Welsh castle-keeps, having three levels, with the entry on the first floor and garde-robe outlets on the first and second floors, the latter of which would have provided the prince and his wife with their main apartment. Intriguingly, the staircase to the second floor reverses its spiral to reach roof level and the now lost battlements.

The low foundations in the courtyard represent a number of drystone buildings: the south tower nearest to the road, a smaller western structure which may too have been a defensive tower, while on the lake side of the rocky summit are the hall and, nearer the keep, a later building probably added by Llywelyn ap Gruffudd.

DOLWYDDELAN

SH 722 523. Cadw. Fee.

• **Access**   South-west of Dolwyddelan village, the castle's square keep still stands guard proudly over the rugged Lledr valley and the A470 by which it can be approached. In fact the medieval road which led from the Conwy valley towards the formidable Crimea pass ran the other side of the castle site. There is a car park, and above it the farmhouse where tickets can be bought, as well as Cadw's joint guidebook to this and Dolbadarn castle. There is a stiff climb to the castle itself.

• **History** Traditionally this was the birthplace of Llywelyn the Great (d.1240), but the event must actually have happened at Tomen Castell nearby, a motte on a knoll close to the river. To that extent the tradition may well be true, since Llywelyn's father Iorwerth ruled only a small part of Gwynedd, including this area. It was almost certainly Llywelyn himself who built the original two-storey keep in this more prominent position, along with its curtain wall. Apart from its strategic position, the site controlled an area noted for the rearing of numerous cattle. The castle has no recorded history, apart from a letter of Llywelyn ap Gruffudd signed here in 1275, until it was besieged and captured by Edward I in January 1283, an event which demonstrates Edward's thoroughness in preparing for winter warfare in such difficult territory; his soldiers were dressed in white as camouflage against the snow.

Dolwyddelan Keep, with 19th-century restored battlements.
Photograph: Paul Davis.

Edward strengthened and extended the buildings, giving command to a loyal Welshman, Griffith ap Tudur; few Englishmen would willingly have taken office in such a remote area. Dolwyddelan played no known rôle in the revolts of Madog or Owain Glyndŵr. It was sold in 1488 by the chamberlain of north Wales to Maredudd ab Ieuan ap Robert, great-grandfather of Sir John Wynn of Gwydir, whose telling of his family history throws much light on this part of Wales. At one time the castle had been the home of Hywel ab Ieuan ap Rhys, an outlaw, and Maredudd faced many problems in what was a lawless area. By the eighteenth century the castle was in ruins, and in 1848 Lord Willoughby de Eresby, whose family had inherited the Gwydir estates, restored the keep to its present condition.

• **Buildings** Llywelyn's builders cut ditches athwart the ridge to provide defences on all four sides, with a bridge where the present causeway reaches the entrance. Llywelyn's keep of local volcanic ash-stone consisted of a basement, with a great chamber above it, provided with a fireplace and separate latrine. The chamber was entered via steps and a drawbridge. There was an oven against the west wall. The third storey was added may have been added by Edward I or later by Maredudd ab Ieuan. The only other accommodation was in the west tower, almost certainly added by Edward I, had a ground-floor entrance and upper chamber with fireplace and latrines.

CARDIGANSHIRE

ABERYSTWYTH

SN579 816. Open access.

• **Access** This sadly wrecked but fascinating site is one of Edward's 1277 ring of castles, which were intended to cow the local Welsh and to contain Llywelyn ap Gruffudd within the Gwynedd rump of his former principality, which had included almost all Ceredigion and most of north and mid-Wales. It is on the seafront, between the Old College and the harbour, where parking can be found. The castle is accessible to wheelchairs. Unfortunately there is no guidebook available.

• **History** The castle of Aberystwyth (estuary of the Ystwyth) is actually on the Rheidol estuary. Known at first as Llanbadarn, after the religious settlement two miles away, the castle and

Aberystwyth Castle gatehouse.

its borough seem eventually to have inherited the name of the **Aberystwyth old castle**, whose fine ringwork and bailey crown the hill above Tanycastell farm at Rhydyfelin (SN 585 790), looking down on the Ystwyth estuary which gave the place its name. This was the work of Gilbert de Clare, the first Norman to seize control of Ceredigion, in 1110. The earthworks are on private land, but can be viewed from the coastal path south of Tan-y-bwlch beach. The gently sloping area south-west of the castle may have been occupied by Gilbert's followers, the Norman equivalent of a Roman *vicus*. Below the steep eastern slope of the castle hill the Normans had built a bridge across the Ystwyth which in 1115 they successfully defended against a marauding Welsh army. North Ceredigion was much fought over by the Normans, the men of Deheubarth and the princes of Gwynedd, and this site was one of the main prizes of frequent battles. The Welsh burnt or captured it in 1136, 1143, 1208, 1210 and 1221.

Edward's 1277 conquest of west and mid-Wales brought the creation of a castle-with-borough on a new site, supervised by his brother Edmund. Most if not all of the castle's skilled workmen were shipped here from Bristol. So was the freestone (now almost vanished) for doorways, while the tough but uncarvable Aberystwyth grits formed the bulk of the masonry. The work was still incomplete when the Welsh rising of Easter 1282 saw it briefly captured and partly destroyed. Work was resumed in 1283 under the initial supervision of Master James of St George, the king's major architect, and completed in 1289, and the castle stood firm against the Welsh rebellion of 1294–95, probably supplied by sea. The twelve years' task had cost at least £4,300.

A century of decay and neglect was followed by the great rebellion of Glyndŵr in 1400, who at his second attempt captured the castle in 1404, using it along with Harlech as a twin centre for his rule over the larger part of Wales. His men were finally evicted in 1408 following the first use in Britain of cannon, but not before one blew up, killing its crew. Further neglect and sea erosion followed, mitigated by occasional repairs, as when Thomas Bushell installed a royal mint here in 1637. The castle endured its final siege in 1646, when the royalists defended it against the parliamentarians for months before surrendering. The castle was ordered to be slighted, the walls blown up and the ruins abandoned.

• **Buildings**   The castle's plan is diamond-shaped and concentric, adapted to the original contours of the site, and must have looked splendid at its best. Its basic shape is that of a double-ringwall, with two gatehouses, and corner-towers to send raking fire along the walls, all built of local gritstone, with dressings of Dundry stone imported by sea. Marine erosion has badly damaged the outer ward, while centuries of neglect and theft of stone have also done their share, not to mention the parliamentarian wrecking. There had also been remodelling in the later medieval period, and later still by Thomas Bushell, who established a silver mint in the castle's hall in 1637, using metal from his Cardiganshire lead-silver mines.

The castle is best entered from the landward side through the original gatehouse, which still has a little of its dignity remaining. The site of the mint is on the left, beyond which the well and a ruined bread-oven can be seen, also on the left. In the remainder of the outer ward beyond the central tower stands the magnificent Aberystwyth war memorial by Mario Rutelli.

Visitors may well be confused by the existence in the courtyard of a large circle of standing stones. Far from being ancient, this monument was erected for the National Eisteddfod of Wales of 1915, postponed till 1916 on account of the Great War, as is briefly noted in Welsh on the side of the large central stone slab. Such modern stone circles are to be found wherever the National Eisteddfod has been held. The counties of Wales were invited each to send a stone from a local quarry, and many of them did so; others bought stone in Ceredigion. The name of each county is inscribed on its stone in the so-called bardic alphabet invented by the creator of the Gorsedd, Iolo Morganwg (1747–1826). The circle is for the ceremonies of the Gorsedd of Bards, and has been used for subsequent Eisteddfodau in 1952 and 1992.

CARDIGAN

SN177 459. Council ownership; occasional access.

• **Access**   Any description of Cardigan Castle is subject to change over the coming years, since the site was in terrible condition when acquired from private ownership by Ceredigion County Council in 2003. Its restoration is bound to be gradual, and access at the time of writing is best arranged by telephoning Ms Jann Tucker at 01239–810387. She is secretary of the Cadwgan Trust which is working with Ceredigion Council to restore the castle. It overlooks the river Teifi and Cardigan bridge; the entrance is along tiny Green Street, leading off Bridge Street.

• **History**   The Norman invaders of 1093 immediately recognised the importance of the Teifi estuary, and a small earthwork castle was built west of the town at Old Castle farm (SN 164 463) by Roger of Montgomery. The Normans reappeared in 1110 and either then or later the present site was occupied and a bridge built. By 1165 Rhys ap Gruffudd (the Lord Rhys) had seized all Ceredigion and began building a stone castle here in 1171; in 1176 he held a competitive festival of music and poetry, known (in retrospect) as the first Eisteddfod. In 1188 he welcomed Archbishop Baldwin of

Cardigan castle in 1741. Samuel and Nathaniel Buck.
Courtesy of the National Library of Wales.

Canterbury to Cardigan on his tour of Wales.

Rhys's death in 1197 led to a renewal of fierce fighting between his sons in which Cardigan ('the key to all Wales') changed hands frequently, including periods in the hands of King John, the Marshall family of Pembroke and Llywelyn the Great. From 1240 it was in the hands of the English, not to be lost again. After the Anglo-Welsh war of 1245 refortification took place, along with the building of town walls around the nascent borough. No serious attacks on the castle took place after that (though during the great revolt of Owain Glyndŵr the castle had to be supplied with food by sea from Bristol in 1404), until 1645 when a royalist garrison put up fierce resistance before finally surrendering to a parliamentarian force. Cromwell ordered the fortifications to be slighted, though part survived to be used as a prison into the eighteenth century.

• **Buildings** The castle was built to command the lowest convenient bridging point on the Teifi, where a natural hillock made the position more easily defensible. Fragments of the medieval curtain walls survive, much augmented by later building as well as a WWII pillbox. Three semicircular towers survive in poor condition; the masonry is yellow sandstone. The keep eventually became part of Castle Green mansion, a complex building partly eighteenth century, partly 1807/8 with later additions, but the keep still bulges out of the rear, and its dungeon was used as a cellar. By the 1980s the house had become so neglected as to be uninhabitable and the owner had moved into a caravan, while trees flourished around and on the ruins. After its purchase by Ceredigion County Council, Cambria Archaeology began excavating and revealed the foundations of the main entry on the western side. The neighbouring cottages, both of which were once inns, were included in the site purchase and have been attractively decorated.

CAER PEN-RHOS *(Llanrhystud) SN 552 695*

TREFILAN *SN 549 571*

• **Access** These two fine Welsh-built earthwork castles make a pleasant joint excursion. Pen-rhos is inland from Llanrhystud on the Ceredigion coast, accessible by footpath from the unclassified road past the Pen-rhos caravan park. Trefilan is on private land right next to the B4337 just north of Tal-sarn, and can be easily viewed from the road, where parking is possible. Between the two the road passes over the slopes of Trichrug, where a short walk gives stunning views and access to three fine Bronze Age tumuli (SN542 599).

Pen-rhos Sometimes indexed as Llanrhystud castle, this splendid hilltop ringwork was built within an Iron Age hill-fort in 1149. It may have been the work of Cadwaladr, brother of Prince Owain Gwynedd, during the period when the men of Gwynedd controlled Ceredigion, but in 1151 it fell to three

Penrhos ringwork. Crown copyright RCAHMW.

of the Lord Rhys's brothers, only to be retaken by the warrior poet and lover of women Hywel ab Owain Gwynedd, who burnt it and slaughtered the garrison. The destruction cannot have been complete, for it came into the possession of Roger de Clare and is mentioned for the last time in 1158. No more than that is known of its history, but at a guess, it may have been supplanted in importance by Trefilan, which became a major administrative centre, while Pen-rhos, though useful militarily, was less convenient.

Trefilan The large mound close to Trefilan church and primary school, next to the B4337, is hardly mentioned in the documentary sources for the period. It was begun by Maelgwn, son of the Lord Rhys, and completed in 1233 by *his* son, Maelgwn Fychan. Trefilan was well-placed to control the Aeron valley, and was almost certainly an important administrative centre for the Welsh rulers of central Ceredigion. When

English forces were mopping up in the summer of 1282 after the Easter rebellion in Ceredigion, they found three thousand cattle gathered at Trefilan, presumably in a Welsh attempt to deny them to the enemy.

CARMARTHENSHIRE

CARMARTHEN

SN 413 200. Council-owned. Free.

• **Access** The wreckage of this major castle used to be hidden behind later housing and the grim County Hall which dominates the town bridge. Years of demolition (criticised by some historians) and restoration have made Carmarthen Castle worth looking at. It is easily accessible on foot, either from the riverside (many steps), or the County Hall entrance, but best from Nott Square, where the gatehouse is a revelation. The ruins can be visited between 10.00am and 4.00pm. The County Council is concerned that until restoration is quite complete, it is not advisable to climb the main tower in wet weather.

• **History** The castle's origins are obscure, depending whether this or somewhere else is the site of Rhyd-y-gors Castle, viciously disputed between Welsh and English in 1095 and 1105. The site is clearly important, the Tywi enabling small ships to penetrate well inland to this good bridging point, dominated by the bluff on which the castle stands. Carmarthen itself is named in 1109; it was burnt by the Welsh in 1137. It is then said to have been rebuilt by Gilbert de Clare in 1145, seized by the Welsh a year later and repaired by them in 1150. However they may have lost it shortly afterwards,

Carmarthen's gatehouse.

because Rhys ap Gruffudd besieged it in 1159 and again on his last rampage in 1196, when he burnt the town but failed to capture the castle. In 1215 Llywelyn ap Iorwerth took the castle and put Maelgwn ap Rhys in charge, but in 1223 it fell to William Marshall, who re-created the castle in stone. Llywelyn sent his son Gruffudd to recover it, but in vain, and although besieged by the Welsh in 1233, it held out. Edward I saw Carmarthen as a key site in controlling south-west Wales, establishing his justiciar there. Carmarthen's importance was emphasised during the revolt of Owain Glyndŵr. His forces captured in 1403 and held it briefly, and in 1405, aided by the

French, the Welsh took possession again, by negotation, but failed to develop it as they did Aberystwyth and Harlech. When recovered by the Crown, serious repairs and reconstruction were necessary.

Edward I made Carmarthen the virtual capital of his principality of south Wales (i.e. most of Carmarthenshire and Cardiganshire), and it retained a central rôle as centre of the south-west circuit of Great Sessions instituted by the Acts of Union. Although those responsibilities have long gone, Carmarthen is still the largest town in south-west Wales. It was a key target during the Civil Wars: captured by Parliament in 1644, recaptured by the Crown, taken again by Parliament in 1646, and although it was ordered to be slighted at least in part, enough remained for it to be converted into the county jail in the eighteenth century.

• **Buildings** Only the western wall, stretching from the shell keep via the fine gatehouse to the south-west round tower and the small square tower a little to the east survive, just enough to remind one of the castle's former status, when it occupied the whole area now filled by County Hall.

CARREG CENNEN

SN 668 191. Cadw. Fee.

• **Access** Only the dead of soul would not thrill to their first view of this mighty eagle's nest, perched on its massive limestone crag in the Cennen valley, in a landscape rich in antiquities: hill-forts (Carn Goch), cairns (Trichrug), pillow mounds and standing stones, as well as place-names (e.g. Faerdre, Rhandir) significant of medieval Welsh land tenure. Deep within the great rock is a cave where human remains have been found under a layer of limestone. At Ffair-fach south of Llandeilo, turn eastwards off the A40, take the first right and up over a steep ridge and down to Trapp. Follow the signs up the narrow road to the car park. Tickets, guidebooks and refreshments are sold in the farmyard building, and a torch to visit the cave can be hired. Pause to see some of the rare-breed sheep and cattle before climbing the cruel slope to this wonderful site.

• **History** The irony of this most Welsh of castle sites is that the visible stonework is entirely of English creation. Its Welsh predecessor, probably built by the Lord Rhys (d.1197), has been entirely swallowed up. At Rhys's death it passed to his son Rhys Gryg (d.1233) and to *his* son Rhys Mechyll (d.1244). This Rhys had married Maud de Braose, of the great Brecon Marcher family and they had a son, yet another Rhys, surnamed Fychan. Maud hated her son and tried to cheat him of his inheritance by delivering it into English hands, but he seized it back in 1248. Thereafter it changed hands several times again in Rhys's feud with his uncle, Maredudd ap Rhys. In 1277 the Welsh lords of the south sided with the king against Llywelyn ap Gruffudd, and Carreg Cennen was handed over to the royal general Pain de Chaworth.

By 1282 the Welsh lords regretted their previous decision; they joined in the great revolt of that year and Carreg Cennen was seized by Gruffudd and Llywelyn, the sons of Rhys Fychan, but their triumph was brief. Edward granted Carreg Cennen to John Giffard, a distinguished soldier and landowner in England, and new buildings were begun, though at what date is not known. In 1287 the castle was captured again by the Welsh during the revolt of Rhys ap Maredudd, once lord of Dinefwr, but his tenure was brief.

A century and more passed before once again the castle was embattled; in 1403 the followers of Owain Glyndŵr attacked when it was held by John Scudamore. He wrote desperately to

Brecon for help, but was forced to surrender to the Welsh, who inflicted such serious damage that £500 had to be spent in repairs when the tumult finally passed. By the mid-fifteenth century the castle was the prop-

The massive remains of Carreg Cennen.

erty of the Duchy of Lancaster, and governed, like much of south-west Wales, by Gruffudd ap Nicholas. In 1461, after the defeat of the Lancastrians at the battle of Mortimer's Cross, Gruffudd's sons had to surrender the castle to Yorkist control and orders were given to dismantle the buildings, clearly unsuccessful. It became the haunt of bats and owls, and over three hundred years later tourists began to frequent it. It was splendidly painted by JMW Turner.

• **Buildings** The steep climb leads to the demolished outer gate then into the outer ward (where stables and workshops probably existed), and on to a long stairway via the barbican, once defended by two drawbridges, past the middle gate tower and left through the gatehouse with portcullis (note the internal defences which would be used against any intruders) into the inner ward. Moving anti-clockwise around the ward, the visitor sees a baking oven, water cisterns, the round north-west tower, then passes the west and south curtain walls to the so-called King's Chamber. Next to this is the domestic and hall area (the hall itself was on the first floor), with the chapel tower beyond it and then to the large north-east tower. All the

85

masonry is of local carboniferous limestone, and the surviving dressings are of sandstone. The cave can be reached via the doorway in the south-east corner. It is steep, damp, dark and can be slippery, so care is needed and a torch essential.

DINEFWR

SN 611 218. National Trust/Cadw. Fee.

• **Access** The splendours of Dinefwr park, mansion and castle are reached from the A40, turning 800 metres south-west of the A40/A483 roundabout. From the National Trust car park there are marked paths to the medieval castle. Alternatively there is a fine walk through bluebell woods from a point above the Towy bridge. The place-name element *din*, a fortification, suggests that there may have been an Iron Age defensive wall on the rock, but no sign of it is visible; the other element, *efwr*, means cow-parsley. The mansion well merits a visit. There is an excellent joint guidebook to Dinefwr and Dryslwyn.

• **History** Dinefwr and its environs form one of the greatest historic landscape sites in Wales. Two Roman forts were identified in the park in 2004, while nearby Llandeilo was a major centre of early Welsh Christianity. The original castle was built well before its first mention in 1163 when Rhys ap Gruffudd seized it from Walter Clifford and made it the major centre of his recently established rule in south-west Wales. Rhys was an astute and effective ruler, known to history as 'the Lord Rhys', but his sons were a turbulent crew who could not wait for their father's death. Maelgwn ap Rhys imprisoned the old warrior in 1194, only for him to be released by a loyal son, Hywel Sais. The following year two more sons seized Dinefwr, but their father captured and imprisoned the pair.

After Rhys's death in 1197 the castle changed hands among

his sons and grandsons, usually bloodily, in 1198, 1204, 1208 and 1213. In 1220 Llywelyn the Great forced Rhys's son, Rhys Gryg, to dismantle part of the castle. Another of Rhys's descendants, Rhys Fychan, carried out reconstruction and established the first local borough, of which nothing remains. By

Dinefwr (courtesy of Ms Diane Mort).

the 1270s another descendant, Rhys ap Maredudd, ruled the Tywi valley. Like most of the Welsh lords who had supported Llywelyn ap Gruffudd in the 1260s and 1270s, Rhys turned against the Welsh prince in 1277, surrendering the castle to the English forces without a fight. In 1282 however, unlike many Welsh lords, Rhys remained loyal to Edward, hoping that the king would restore Dinefwr to him. Meanwhile the English had repaired Dinefwr and used it as a centre in the war of 1282–83. Disappointed of his hopes, Rhys raised a revolt against the Crown in 1287, briefly seizing Dinefwr, but his efforts failed, and he was eventually betrayed and executed.

The castle was sacked in 1321 in the civil war of Edward II; restored, it was besieged unsuccessfully by Glyndŵr's rebels in 1403. Finally Sir Rhys ap Thomas, major supporter of Henry VII at Bosworth in 1485, moved from the castle to the site now occupied by the mansion of his descendant Sir Edward Rice.

Building It takes longer to reach the castle than to enjoy it, but the signed paths are most attractive. They unite to approach the castle's only entrance, crossing a rock-cut ditch to reach the virtually destroyed outer bailey and passing through the site of the old gateway into the barbican, thus reaching the present gateway. This gives access to a walled five-sided courtyard, dominated by the massive round keep, mostly of early or mid-thirteenth-century date and now crowned with the previously-mentioned summer-house; the round north-west tower is slightly later. The masonry is of Llandeilo flagstone, with sandstone dressings. On the north-east side the original curtain wall was destroyed, possibly at the command of Llywelyn the Great. It was replaced, perhaps by Rhys ap Maredudd, with a chamber block close to the keep, and an adjoining hall was added, probably by Hugh le Despenser before 1321. These buildings, together with the smaller round tower, were later modified by Sir Rhys ap Thomas before he abandoned the old castle in favour of the present mansion's site.

The ground-floor entrance to the round keep is a modern device; the only entrance to the tower would have been up a now-vanished flight of stairs; access to the basement would have been from above by trap-door. Contrary to popular belief, many such castle basements were not used as dungeons but for storage. Part of the curtain wall which would have surrounded the keep on its north-east side has fallen away. From the towers there are splendid views in every direction; the finest is to the west down the Tywi valley, where Paxton's Tower, Dryslwyn Castle and Grongar Hill can all be seen in clear weather. Note also the ox-bow pools, the former course of the river Tywi, beneath the castle.

DRYSLWYN

SN 554 204. Cadw. Open access.

• **Access** The castle is best reached from the A40; the signed turning is some four miles west of Llandeilo. There is a convenient car park, but no easy way of reaching the castle except by the steep path up this massive hump of carboniferous limestone, however the views alone are worth the effort. It would have been much harder for the besiegers of 1287.

• **History** Dryslwyn's early history is apparently undocumented until 1271, when its lord Maredudd ap Rhys Gryg, grandson of Rhys ap Gruffudd, died there. It can be presumed to have been built by Maredudd or his father in the mid- or early thirteenth century; whether Rhys ap Gruffudd built here is not known. There is no sign of prehistoric or early medieval occupation on the site. Maredudd's son, another Rhys, sided with Edward I in the war of 1282/3, but disappointed of his hopes of regaining his hereditary Dinefwr lands, he rebelled

Dryslwyn Keep above the vale of Tywi.

in 1287 and withstood siege in the castle. The siege must have been dramatic; trebuchets hurled huge stones at the walls while 11,000 men assembled in the valley ready for the assault. Attempts at undermining the walls killed many of the attackers, including the Earl of Stafford. The siege lasted a month, at the end of which (if not earlier), Rhys ap Maredudd managed to escape. After five years on the run he was caught and executed. The new constable, Alan Plukenet, spent money on repairs and a new mill nearby. This was part of the development of a pre-existing Welsh borough described below. Excavations revealed numerous arrowheads, slingstones and a menacing mace-head. Owain Glyndŵr's forces succeeded in capturing Dryslwyn in 1403 and the borough may have been destroyed and abandoned. Nothing is known of the castle's later history.

• **Buildings** The footpath up the hill eventually reaches the town ditch within which the town walls once stood two metres high, and where a gatehouse stood. Humps, bumps and crude terraces are what remains of this early Welsh borough, which failed for obvious reasons. There were at least 34 houses here, as well as other buildings, all for the use of the garrison and their families and horses. The castle was entered by a large gatehouse of which only the foundations survive, and a guest of the castle in its heyday would pass through the outer and middle wards, full of activity, to the inner gate. Excavation has shown that there was a good deal of thirteenth-century remodelling of this and other parts of the castle.

Once through the gate, the great Welsh keep, its walls three metres thick, is followed by a complexity of domestic buildings including the east hall, the foundations of the great hall and beyond them a chapel, kitchen and apartment block, as well as a small prison cell and a latrine. Today this accommodation looks bleak indeed, the flagstone masonry deprived of all its dressings and timber, but excavation has shown that the castle's occupants, notably Rhys ap Maredudd and his father, lived in considerable comfort. Rooms were plastered, at least some windows were glazed, river and sea fish and meat formed the base of the diet, along with bread, as well as figs and raisins.

KIDWELLY

SN 409 070. Cadw. Fee.

• **Access** With the creation of a by-pass Kidwelly has reverted to its traditional sleepy air of a medieval borough that, despite its tin-works, didn't seem to want to compete with its upstart neighbour Llanelli. Its splendid castle deserves to be much better known. Most visitors will approach from Carmarthen; turn off the A484 by-pass and look out for signs on the left, easily missed, or choose the agreeable free car park on the right by the river bridge, from which a pleasant footpath takes you beside the Gwendraeth to the castle and its visitor centre. It has an excellent Cadw guidebook. Plays are performed in the castle in the summer months. The priory church is usually open to visitors.

• **History** The Welsh commote of Cydweli is the area between the estuaries of the Tywi and the Gwendraeth Fach. The castle site was chosen because it guarded the lowest bridging point on the Gwendraeth, but the little town founded beneath its ramparts at the behest of Henry I eventually spread across the river and grew there, leaving the castle behind. With the Welsh uprising of 1136 Gruffudd ap Rhys, titular prince of Deheubarth, went north to seek help from his brothers-in-law of Gwynedd, while his wife Gwenllian led an army to capture Kidwelly. Alas, the only Welsh woman military leader was defeated and killed at Maes Gwenllian, north of the castle, by

Kidwelly's complex plan is best understood from the air.
Crown copyright RCAHMW.

English forces led by Maurice de Londres.

Maurice and his descendants lost their hold on the castle in 1159 and 1190 to Rhys ap Gruffudd, and a third time to his son Rhys Gryg in 1215. It was returned to Hawise, the de Londres heiress in 1220, who held it in the teeth of Llywelyn ap Iorwerth's sweep through the south in 1231. With the lordship the castle passed in 1274 to her sons Pain (d.1279) and Patrick de Chaworth (d.1283). During their tenure much of the present fabric was built, transforming it into one of the first rank of Marcher castles.

After a period in the hands of William de Valence (d.1296), uncle to Edward I, Kidwelly passed to the king's nephew Henry, earl of Lancaster, who had married the Chaworth heiress. Thence it graduated, via Henry's granddaughter Blanche, wife of John of Gaunt, into kingly ownership, since Henry's great-grandson became Henry IV in 1399. A good deal of building, not easily dated, went on during these years, culminating in the splendid gatehouse, all making the castle worthy of its ownership by the great Lancaster family and its use as an important administrative centre. Richard II was the last royal visitor here, in May 1399, the year of his abdication and murder.

Building work was still in hand when in 1403 Henry Don, a prominent local Welsh gentleman, joined the Glyndŵr rebellion and attacked Kidwelly. The town fell, but the castle held out for months before Don abandoned the siege, and was eventually pardoned. Building work on the castle was resumed and continued for eighteen years, with a long record of subsequent repairs, but these were not enough to maintain such a large complex whose importance was much reduced; by 1600 it was much decayed. Indeed, Kidwelly had become such a backwater that it was not involved in the Civil Wars. Eventually the castle passed to the earls of Cawdor, the greatest landowners of south-west Wales, and in 1927 it became government property.

• **Buildings** Within a comparatively small area Kidwelly contains most of the typical features of a medieval stone castle; equally typical is the long span of time during which they were altered or destroyed and rebuilt. It is an interesting example of the kind of concentric castle perfected at Beaumaris, its plan affected by the nature of the site high above the river Gwendraeth.

The gatehouse, with its doorway recessed between the towers, and with three archlike machicolations high above, bears a close resemblance to Carmarthen; it was completed in 1422. There was a complex array of defences: drawbridge, arrow-slits, portcullis and a murder hole, as well as the machicolations from which boulders could be dropped, none of which was ever tested in war. Inside is a complex of twenty rooms, with a dungeon in the east tower only accessible through a hole in the floor.

From the gatehouse one enters the outer ward which is contained on the west by a massive curved curtain wall with walkway reaching round to the collapsed north gate; it includes the two fine bakehouse ovens. On the right is the rectangular inner ward with four fine towers. Against the east wall is the hall range for which a kitchen was provided on the west side of the ward, next to the south-west tower, which like the keep at Pembroke still has its vaulted roof, a rare feature.

Protruding from the south-east tower, which contained the best accommodation, is the chapel tower; the piscina for washing the sacred vessels and the sedilia (priests' seats) are clearly visible from below (see p.26). The castle's stonework includes riverstones, millstone grit and carboniferous limestone, with dressings in old red sandstone.

LAUGHARNE

SN 303 107. Cadw. Fee.

• **Access**   Laugharne lies on the A4066 about 4 kilometres south of St Clears, itself accessible from both east and west via the A40. It is a one-street, picturesque village with the castle at the end of the main street before it turns down to sea level, and car parking at the foot of the small promontory on which the building stands. Laugharne is enormously popular with summer visitors, whether or not they are on the Dylan Thomas trail; the fine parish church, where the poet is buried, warrants a visit when open. There is an excellent Cadw guidebook.

• **History**   Three rivers flow into Carmarthen Bay, with Laugharne guarding the estuary of the Taf. Before problems

Laugharne Castle. Crown copyright RCAHMW.

of silting made it impossible, medieval and early modern shipping used the little port; merchants' houses can still be seen opposite the car park, and the town has retained its medieval government headed by the port-reeve.

The original ringwork castle here seems to have been established in 1116 by Robert Courtemain, who entrusted its care to a Welshman, Bleddyn ap Cedifor. Its first role in history was as a meeting-place for Henry II with the Lord Rhys in 1171–72, one of at least two meetings where the two enemies buried the hatchet and Rhys became the king's justiciar in south-west Wales. When Henry died in 1189 the Anglo-Welsh truce was broken and Rhys captured St Clears, Llansteffan and Laugharne castles, when Laugharne may have been burnt. The refurbished castle was in English hands by 1215, when Llywelyn the Great, aided by the Lord Rhys's sons, swept through the south, seizing Laugharne and a number of other castles. Badly damaged, it eventually came back into the hands of William Marshall.

By 1247 Laugharne had been granted to Guy de Brian IV, head of a western English family. At first his life may have been quiet, but in 1257 Llywelyn ap Gruffudd rampaged through south-west Wales, destroying Laugharne castle and town, capturing de Brian and holding him for ransom. Before his death about 1268 de Brian had done much to shape the castle in its later form. His son Guy V continued the work and granted Laugharne its borough charter. Guy VII (d.1390), a fine soldier and civil servant to Edward III, strengthened the castle and improved its accommodation.

The castle became subject to inheritance disputes for many years; it was reinforced in 1403 for fear of Owain Glyndŵr, but was left alone by the rebels. In 1488 it became the property of the Earl of Northumberland and in 1585, of Sir John Perrot, who found it a ruin and did his best to convert it to a Tudor mansion, as he did at Carew. After his death in the Tower of London in 1592, Laugharne passed through successive ownerships. It was under parliamentarian control in 1644, but was captured by the royalist general Sir Charles Gerard, only to be lost again after a weeklong siege, after which much of the castle was slighted. It changed ownership several more times, with much of the site eventually turned into a garden. The last private owners, the Starke family, did some restoration work in the 1930s and rented the castle to the novelist Richard Hughes, who lived in Castle House and wrote his second novel *In Hazard* (1938) in the gazebo, a place also favoured by his friend Dylan Thomas. It was given to the Welsh Office in 1973.

• **Buildings** The spacious outer ward, nicely gardened, is roughly diamond-shaped, with the main castle of red sandstone neatly tucked into the southern corner on the low bluff edge. Most of the outer curtain walls are recent, following the line of the medieval defences. Visitors enter through the late thirteenth century outer gatehouse and face two massive thirteenth century towers, the one on the left largely destroyed, the two linked by Perrot's three-storey range with fine central stair tower.

To the right the inner gatehouse gives entry to the inner ward. On the right are the basements of the kitchen range with a huge chimney and of the hall, with the well close by. The kitchen had a stone floor resting on vaulting. The complexities of the whole building are well illustrated by the south-west tower: the base is thirteenth century, mid-section is fourteenth century greenstone, and the upper part is of the late sixteenth century. Do not miss the fine view of the castle from the car park and footpath below.

LLANDOVERY

SN 767 343. Open access.

• **Access** No urban castle in Wales is better provided with parking facilities (at a price) than Llandovery, right in the town centre. The mound rises virtually from the tarmac, and access is free at all times. A pity there is so little left, but enjoy the excellent Visitors' Centre close by.

• **History** Ten centuries before the Normans their Roman predecessors had recognised this site between the rivers Bran, Gwydderig and Tywi as strategically valuable, and so they built a fort half a mile north of the castle site. It was a road hub with routes running east to Brecon, south-west to Llandeilo and NNE to mid-Wales, and the Normans certainly needed good communications as they attempted to break the stubborn resistance of the Welsh in the heart of this region of Deheubarth. It was from Brecon that they had forced their way into the Tywi valley.

The original castle was the work of Richard fitz Pons in 1116 or earlier, but he put it in the charge of a cooperative local Welsh leader who defended it fiercely against Welsh siege. It passed to Walter Clifford, but in 1158 Rhys ap Gruffudd stormed and took the castle, and then rebuilt it. After his death his sons fought savagely over their father's lands; this castle changed hands five times between 1200 and 1204. It remained in Welsh hands until 1277, when it was taken by John Giffard, who refurbished the building and held it in the king's name. In the great revolt of Easter 1282 Llandovery fell to Llywelyn ap Gruffudd's brother Dafydd, aided by local assault, but stayed in Welsh hands only briefly. However, the discontented descendant of Rhys ap Gruffudd, Rhys ap Maredudd, rose in revolt in 1287 and briefly set the Tywi valley aflame, seizing Llandovery among other castles, but his rebellion was short-lived.

The castle was not abandoned by its eventual lords, the Audley family, and was quickly put into commission against Glyndŵr's rebellion. In 1401 it was the scene of the hanging of a leading Welsh squire and Glyndŵr sympathiser, Llywelyn ap Gruffudd Fychan, on the orders and in the presence of Henry IV; Llywelyn had deliberately led the English troops in the wrong direction, and it is he who is commemorated by the large stainless steel figure erected on the motte. Despite Glyndŵr's successes in south Wales, Llandovery did not fall to his attacks. Eventually it fell into ruin, and many of its stones are certainly incorporated in the houses nearby. Llandovery was given its borough charter in 1485 by Richard III.

Llywelyn ap Gruffydd Fychan's extraordinary memorial at Llandovery.

Description. The motte, though eroded by generations of feet, is still formidable in size, but only fragments are left of a SW tower, a small west tower and some walling, all in local sandstone.

LLANSTEFFAN

SN 351 101. Cadw. Open access.

• **Access** This magnificent ruin clearly suffers a shortage of visitors because of its position. Its dominant outline may attract motorists to drive straight towards it from Llansteffan, but there is no parking except by the beach, which is reached by keeping left as one comes to the village. The ruins are a pleasant mile-long walk from the village or half-a-mile from the beach. No castle-lover should miss it. There is a good Cadw leaflet available in the village post-office opposite the fine church.

• **History** This splendid hilltop site with views over the Tywi and Gwendraeth estuaries as far as Gower, and westwards on a clear day to Pembrokeshire, was used in the pre-Roman centuries to build a hill-fort. The Normans saw its advantages equally clearly and created a ringwork here soon after 1100. The sheltered beach below became a shipping haven and the little borough flourished on trade.

In 1146 the castle was captured and held for a while by the grandsons of Rhys ap Tewdwr (d.1093), last king of south-west Wales. They repelled a Norman attack, successfully throwing the scaling ladders back from the timber walls, but eventually abandoned the site; before 1200 it was granted to scions of the de Camville family. The Welsh did not give up easily; it was stormed and taken in 1189 (by the Lord Rhys, one of the successful besiegers of 1146), in 1215 (by Llywelyn the Great) and in 1257 by the Lord Rhys's great-grandson Rhys Fychan. Each time it was eventually restored to the current de Camville, and subsequent improvements were made. The last de Camville died in 1338, and the lordship passed to the Penres family of Gower. Llansteffan suffered its last successful capture in 1405–6 when taken by Owain Glyndŵr's followers.

Llansteffan: the gatehouse seen from the ward, looking north.

It reverted to Crown ownership, and for a while was possessed by Jasper Tudor, uncle of Henry VII. Thereafter it fell into ruin, and eventually became government property in 1959.

• **Buildings** The steep approach originally led to the late thirteenth-century great gatehouse, but its entrance was blocked by Jasper Tudor and the present simple entry was made; the gatehouse itself became domestic accommodation. Turning right in the lower ward, the visitor will find modern steps leading up to the now roofless first floor hall, with fine carvings high on the right. The floor rests on the vaulted ceiling of the original gateway. It still has several murder holes and the slots for two portcullises, which normally would have been in lowered position and therefore not a nuisance to occupants of the hall. In the further right-hand corner is a flight of steps to the highest point of the ruins, with splendid views in all directions.

Returning to the lower ward, one may walk back past the gatehouse to the strong north tower and on to the Tudor barn and the east bastion. Then follow the curtain wall to the circular foundation of a tower. This stands on the original line of the inner ward's north curtain wall, now largely destroyed. The main ruin here is that of the original square gatehouse of the early thirteenth century; to its left are substantial half-cellular ruins whose purpose is unknown. The well is clearly visible in the inner ward.

NEWCASTLE EMLYN

SN 311 407. Open access.

• **Access** Since this little town is based on a single street and the castle is adequately signed, and moreover there is a free car park at the end of the lane with a display panel about the castle, access is easy, at least for the able-bodied.

• **History** A 'new castle' in the *cantref* or district of Emlyn south of the Teifi is first mentioned in 1215, when it was captured by Llywelyn the Great, and possibly abandoned. About 1240 Maredudd ap Rhys Gryg built here in stone, having realised how easy it would be to defend a height nearly surrounded by a river and steep slopes. After Maredudd's death in 1271 it became by 1277 the property of the Hastings family of Abergavenny, whose daughter Ada married Maredudd's son Rhys in 1285, with Newcastle Emlyn as her dowry. But after Rhys's rebellion of 1287–8, royal forces captured the castle aided by a large catapult; Rhys was caught and executed.

The castle was stormed by Owain Glyndŵr's followers in 1403; eventually it became a domestic residence, with suitable alterations, for Sir Rhys ap Thomas, ally of Henry VII. In the Civil War a royalist garrison defended it in 1644, creating defensive earthworks on the approaches to the castle, but surrendering after a fortnight's siege, after which the parliamentary authorities ordered the castle to be slighted.

Newcastle Emlyn's west-facing gatehouse.

• **Building** The only approach by land is from the car park to the west, through an outer ward. Facing the visitor is the gatehouse of 1321 with its curtain walls, the best surviving masonry on the site, probably the work of Crown agents on behalf of Edward II. To the south is a corner tower with curtain walling, and to the north are the remains of a corner turret with the chute of the garderobe still in place.

DENBIGHSHIRE

CHIRK

SJ 268 381. National Trust. Fee.

• **Access** This splendidly emparked castle lies west of Chirk village, itself on the A5 between Oswestry and Wrexham, and is well signposted. Before reaching the castle the traveller is confronted by the fabulous wrought iron gates made by the Davies brothers in the early eighteenth century. The original home farm is now a visitor centre. The forbidding bulk of the castle on its low hill is approached from the car park on foot, though there is a minibus for needy visitors. Chirk is open from mid-March to the end of October (not Monday or Tuesday). Guidebook. The Poncysyllte aqueduct is not far away.

• **History** Chirk has been continuously occupied since medieval times. Edward I gave the Chirk lands of Llewelyn Fychan to Roger Mortimer, who began building in the 1290s. After the fall in 1330 of his nephew, also Roger Mortimer, it passed to the Fitzalans, Earls of Arundel. Chirk was seized by Richard II in 1396 and made part of his principality of Chester, but after Richard's death the Chirklanders joined in Owain Glyndŵr's revolt, not submitting to Henry IV until 1406, yet the castle seems to have survived unscathed. It passed through the hands of Richard III, of Sir William Stanley, Sir Thomas Seymour and Robert, earl of Leicester before its purchase in 1595 by Sir Thomas Myddleton. Six of the earlier owners died violent deaths.

Sir Thomas Myddleton was a major figure in the London world of finance, lord mayor of London in 1613 and co-founder of the East India Company. He helped finance the first popular edition of the Bible in Welsh (1630), a copy of which is on show in the castle, before dying a year later. His eldest

Chirk from the south-east.

son, also Sir Thomas, supported the parliamentarian cause in the Civil Wars and found himself in 1644–45 attempting to recapture his own castles of Chirk and Ruthin which had been seized by royalists, though he abstained from siege warfare in hope of regaining his own property undamaged, and succeeded through bribery. In 1659 however he declared prematurely for Charles II, and a parliamentarian army besieged, captured and slighted the castle severely. Instead of abandoning the ruin Myddleton spent £30,000 of subsequent compensation on rebuilding. Further extensive alterations were made in the eighteenth and nineteenth centuries, in the latter period by Augustus Pugin, to whom an exhibition is dedicated in the castle. In 1801 Chirk passed by a Myddleton heiress to the Biddulph family, and descendants adopted the Myddleton name. The castle was given to the National Trust in 1974, but the Myddletons still retain an apartment within the buildings.

• **Buildings** There is a remarkable contrast between Chirk's grim exterior and its lush apartments. Mortimer's original castle was planned as a massive rectangle with colossal drum towers, four at the corners and half-towers midway on the south, east and west walls. Since the towers were never completed to plan, they rise no higher than the curtain walls, adding to their squat and menacing bulk, although they have windows from later periods which alleviate their appearance. Only five original towers and the north gateway survived the Civil War slighting; four of those have modified interiors, while the fifth, the south-west or Adam's tower, retains much of its medieval nature, complete with deep dungeon.

Chirk's mighty towers may be perceived as a military statement, but there was no outer curtain wall as at Beaumaris, with which it is sometimes compared, nor is there a moat, while the gateway is remarkably simple when compared with those of the Edwardian castles. The original courtyard must have seemed claustrophobic; today it is much improved by huge climbing plants. There is the usual excellent Trust tearoom in the north range, which also provides entry for visitors to the splendid tour of the stately interior.

DENBIGH

SJ 051 657. Cadw. Fee.

• **Access** Although this fine castle is perched high in the middle of a well-known town and has a car park, it is more easily reached on foot (if you can manage the steep approach) than by car, since the lanes up the hill to the car park are narrow and twisting. The A543 runs through the old town, and if coming from the east, visitors will find a car park near the top of the hill (Vale Street); if full, another one (long-term) is signposted. Walk up Vale Street to the nearby tourist centre (worth a brief visit) and keep left round this building to find Bull Lane, which wriggles its way up past the gate to the fine medieval town walls (ask for the key at the tourist office) and the castle. The castle is open and free during the winter, but admission is charged during the summer. From mid-May to the end of August a number of performances are staged in the castle, from Shakespeare to demonstrations of medieval warfare.

• **History** The Welsh name *Dinbych* means a little fortress, and no doubt there was an Iron Age defence on this fine hill. However the first motte-and-bailey in the area may have been Llys Gwenllian, a mile SSE of Denbigh. The hill was fortified in the twelfth or thirteenth century by one of the Welsh princes, but by whom is not known; it is surprising that such a splendid position had not been used by Robert of Rhuddlan in the eleventh century. Dafydd ap Gruffudd, Llywelyn's brother and enemy, became its tenant after Edward I's victory in the 1276–77 war, having been generously rewarded for his help. However there is no record of Edward making any building payments as he did for Dafydd's new castle at Caergwrle.

Denbigh castle. Crown copyright RCAHMW.

When Dafydd raised his revolt at Easter 1282 it met with some initial success, but Edward was in no mood for any further compromise with contumacious Welsh princes. He personally led the northernmost of three armies into Wales, marching with heavy deliberation to the Clwyd valley, where he captured Denbigh in the autumn of that year. He gave the lordship of Denbigh to Henry de Lacy, Earl of Lincoln, and commissioned him to build a new and splendid castle, with a new walled borough attached. Lacy also created a deer park. The castle may not have been completed when Madog ap Llywelyn's revolt of 1294 saw the Welsh seize the castle, but once again Edward's military machine proved too strong. The castle remained an administrative centre for many years, and seems to have had no serious involvement in the Glyndŵr rebellion. In 1460 it was defended by Yorkist forces in the Wars of the Roses, and taken by Jasper Tudor, uncle of the future king Henry VII. It last appears in history in the Civil Wars. In late 1645 Charles I was forced to take refuge in the castle, commanded by Colonel William Salesbury. After a four months' siege and the king's flight Salesbury gave up his determined but hopeless defence at Charles's express command.

• **Buildings** There is now no trace of the earlier Welsh castle on the site. The plan is oval with no outer ward, simply an inner ward originally surrounded by high curtain walls. The visitor is confronted by the magnificent triple-towered Great Gatehouse, almost certainly built to the design of Master James, who is known to have worked here. The entrance passage is complex; originally one passed through a defended passageway, under two 'murder holes' in the roof vault and under a portcullis. There was then a door defended by arrowslits on either side, then a second portcullis. On the left is the porter's lodge tower, on the right the prison tower, and then the hall is reached. Beyond this is the Badnes tower, which provided good accommodation for the constable of the castle and distinguished guests. Passage from the hall to the inner ward was barred by yet another portcullis and double door. The masonry is carboniferous limestone, with dressings of Cefn sandstone.

Circling the walls clockwise from the Badnes tower, the visitor passes the Great Kitchen tower, the wrecked foundations of the Great Hall, the White Chamber tower and the ruined Green Chambers. Beyond this is the Postern tower, where the town walls join the castle. Then there is a steep passage down from the upper gate, defended by a barbican. Next come the Mantlets, a series of defended areas below the main castle wall, intended to defend the castle's weaker flank. The remaining towers are respectively the Treasure House tower and a subordinate tower, the Bishop's tower and the Red tower. At this point the town walls recommence. Near the Green Chambers are the foundations of a pigeon house, intended to supply fresh meat all the year round for the garrison.

The town walls, well worth a visit, are unusual in that whereas the other walled towns of Wales – Conwy, Caernarfon, Tenby – are still full of houses and shops, the original burgesses who dwelt within the bastide eventually found the steepness of the site difficult and the protection of the walls unnecessary, so they gradually migrated down the hill to the present town centre, leaving the old borough virtually empty. They even abandoned their church, St Hilary's, of which only the tower remains, while the Earl of Leicester's attempt to build a cathedral lower down the hill to replace St Asaph's failed utterly, though ruins remain.

DINAS BRÂN

SJ 222 430. Open access.

• **Access** Perched higher than almost any other castle in Britain, visible for miles around, Dinas Brân is romantic in appearance but a tough one to reach. The stout of limb and lungs will climb from Llangollen bridge, a fierce and long ascent; the rest may get some way up by car along rugged and unclassified lanes, but even so the last half-mile walk is steep; the princes who used it must have depended greatly on their horses. There are Cadw display panels on site. A visit to Valle Crucis abbey nearby makes the trip even more worthwhile.

• **History** Whichever path he takes the climber will cross the rampart and ditch of an Iron Age hill-fort to reach Dinas Brân's shattered remains. Although it must have been a substantial castle, its history was brief. It was built probably by Gruffudd ap Madog (d.1269), an erstwhile ally of Henry III and ruler of northern Powys, who gave his allegiance to Llywelyn ap Gruffudd when the king sought to divide that realm between Gruffudd and his three brothers. In May 1277, on the approach of the royal army under the Earl of Lincoln, the garrison burnt the castle and retreated, leaving the site in English hands. Either during or before his revolt of 1282 Dafydd ap Gruffudd, Llywelyn's brother, had taken possession of the castle and it had to be taken by the English a second time. It was granted to the Earl of Surrey, and disappears from history, but not from romance.

The medieval tale of Foulk Fitzwarin tells how the castle ruins were believed to be haunted. A Norman knight, Paine Peveril, and his followers decide to spend the night there. They are attacked by the giant Gogmagog, whom Paine stabs, and the dying brute tells of how he had driven the castle's builder, 'King Bran', from the mountain and terrorised the country, and of buried treasure on the site.

Dinas Brân dominated its landscape spectacularly.

The castle is the subject of a well-known and atmospheric Welsh verse:

> *Englyn a thelyn a thant – a'r gwleddoedd*
> *Arglwyddawl ddarfuant;*
> *Lle bu bonedd Gwynedd gant*
> *Adar nos a deyrnasant.*   (Taliesin o Eifion)

Poetry, harp and song,
and the lordly feasts are finished;
Where roistered the rulers of Gwynedd,
birds of the night now rule.

• **Buildings** Dinas Brân is a rectangular castle, reminiscent in plan of Dolforwyn, but much simpler. Its gatehouse is at the north-east corner; the curtain walls lack other corner towers, but the gatehouse approach is protected by a projecting oblong keep. There was a projecting apsidal tower in the south wall which may have been part of the castle hall. The massive ditch to south and east clearly provided the building materials.

RUTHIN

SJ 124 579. Hotel.

• **Access** Ruthin Castle is easily reached from the town centre simply by turning along Castle Street for a short distance and then entering the Ruthin Castle Hotel grounds. The hotel, which looks quite castle-like, is a nineteenth-century fantasy added on to a medieval castle; part of the ruined gatehouse can be seen on the right close to the entrance to the drive. The castle can only be accessed by prior arrangement with the hotel staff (tel: 01824 702664) and a member of staff has to escort visitors, since gates have to be unlocked and relocked. I was given every cooperation on my visit. Ruthin's splendid collegiate church is also well worth seeing.

• **History** Ruthin sits on a ridge of red sandstone which simply invited a castle to be built on it, but none is known before 1277, though Llywelyn the Great may have had a court there. When Edward I rolled back the frontier of independent Gwynedd to the river Conwy in that year his ditchers began work on the site, but he granted the lordship to Llywelyn ap Gruffudd's treacherous brother Dafydd as a reward for his support. Whether Edward then commissioned Dafydd to begin a castle is not entirely clear, though it is possible that a small Welsh castle was partly incorporated into the later building.

Ruthin: splendidly overgrown and unrestored.

What is certain is that after Dafydd's rebellion in 1282 Edward granted Dyffryn Clwyd to Reginald de Grey, justiciar of Chester, who built a massive stone castle supervised by James of St George, with an attached borough.

Reginald's descendant, another Reginald de Grey, brought disaster not only on himself but on English rule in Wales for a decade. One of the few independent Welsh noblemen of princely descent, Owain Glyndŵr, had a home in the Dee valley between Llangollen and Corwen. By the year 1400 there was great discontent over much of Wales, and English officials were loathed. The deposition of Richard II in 1399 did not help; a usurper, Henry Bolingbroke had taken the throne, and the time was ripe for revolt. Grey provoked his Welsh neighbour, Owain Glyndŵr, who having had himself proclaimed Prince of Wales, assaulted Ruthin castle and burnt the town on 16 September 1400. Grey and the castle survived the attack, but many of his neighbours did not, and in 1402 Grey himself was captured, imprisoned at Dolwyddelan and only released on payment of ten thousand marks (£6,666, a colossal sum). Thus impoverished, the Greys eventually sold the castle in 1508.

Ruthin was held for Charles I against parliament in 1646, but Thomas Mytton successfully besieged the castle and much of the stonework was pulled down, the site becoming a quarry. The ruin was bought by the Myddleton-West family, who built a mansion partly within the lower bailey in 1826. From 1849 the mansion was recreated in baronial castle style, and many travellers down the Denbigh–Ruthin road must imagine that the impressive red tower they see above the trees must be the medieval castle. It is in fact part of the mansion, now a splendidly luxurious hotel.

• **Buildings**   At the time of writing there is no printed guidebook to Ruthin castle. The serious visitor would be well-advised to read the excellent Castles of Wales website (www.castlewales.com) account by John Northall, which includes reconstruction drawings. This is useful because the ravages of time and the alterations of gardeners have left an intriguing but confusing site, with much of the sandstone masonry still hidden by luxuriant vegetation. The site itself was divided from the borough by the lord's garden; there were ponds, with an orchard and deer park – a truly lordly landscape.

There are two parts to the castle, the upper bailey (inner ward) originally accessed by a gateway near the present hotel entrance, and the lower bailey, separated from the upper by a massive dry moat. The upper bailey is pentagonal, with the site of the hall on the far side from the gate. The twin towers of the gatehouse, though sadly wrecked, still have their vaulted basements. The lower bailey had a main gate entrance into the dry moat. Not far from this gate was a small sally-port from which defenders could counter-attack. The three towers of this long wall give splendid views, and the wall itself, though somewhat dilapidated and draped with greenery, is hugely impressive. A visit may be completed with coffee or tea in the hotel.

SYCHARTH

SJ 205 258. Private land with public access.

• **Access** This iconic and numinous site is difficult to find in a network of tiny roads south-west of Oswestry without an OS map. It has been made easily accessible from the road and layby through cooperation between Cadw and the owners, the Wynnstay Estate.

Sycharth's splendid earthworks.
Crown copyright RCAHMW.

• **History and Site.** Were it not for Iolo Goch's famous poem to Owain Glyndŵr at Sycharth it would be hard to believe that this Norman motte was still in use in the 1390s. There is no trace on the splendid mound of the fine timber hall nor of other buildings in the bailey which Iolo described as being like shops in London. However Iolo's fishpond is still to be seen below the site. Owain was lord of the eastern half of the commote of Cynllaith, a rich fragment of the kingdom of Powys of whose royal family he was the principal male descendant. He held other lands: Glyndyfrdwy between Corwen and Llangollen, and Iscoed in Cardiganshire, but Sycharth was his principal centre. Barely a mile from today's English border, it was quickly lost to Owain when burnt by Prince Henry in 1403 on a punishment raid and never reoccupied.

TOMEN Y RHODWYDD

SJ 177 516. Private land; permission available.

TOMEN Y FAERDRE

SJ 193 561. Private land, permission available.

• **Access** These two fine mottes, one certainly and one possibly of Welsh origin, are close to the village of Llanarmon-yn-Iâl. For the first, follow the A525 from Ruthin towards Wrexham, but turn left (B5431) for Llanarmon-yn-Iâl. The motte is visible on left, with access across a caravan park; permission available at the farmhouse. For the second, follow the A494 towards Mold, turn right on the B5430 towards Llanarmon, then right on the B5431. The motte is on the left before the bridge; permission at farmhouse opposite the east end of the church.

• **History and Sites.** Llanarmon is an ancient village centred

Tomen y Rhodwydd. Crown copyright RCAHMW.

on a fine church often open to visitors, and is named for Saint Garmon who routed the fifth-century followers of the Pelagian heresy in north-east Wales, and for the lordship of Yale (Welsh *Iâl*). The name **Y Faerdre** means a demesne or lordship farm worked by bondmen of the Welsh prince or lord, and suggests a court or Welsh administrative centre, though whether the ditched motte is of Welsh origin cannot be known for certain. It surely predates the vigorous appearance of King John in north-east Wales but may have been strengthened at his command.

Tomen y Rhodwydd is certainly Welsh in origin; Owain Gwynedd (d.1170) built this fine motte-and-bailey in 1149 to confirm his annexation of part of northern Powys. Aided by Henry II's invasion of 1157, Iorwerth Goch of Powys recaptured it, but his hold may have been brief. Both castles were taken by King John in his 1211–12 Welsh campaign. Welsh *rhod* means a circle; the name refers to the castle's plan.

FLINTSHIRE

CAERGWRLE

SJ 307 572. Open access.

• **Access** The castle was once known as Hope, because it was
the centre of Hope lordship, but it stands above Caergwrle
village, and that is now the usual name. Caergwrle can be
reached along the A541 from Wrexham, or by following signs
from the A550 Hawarden road at a junction immediately west
of a railway bridge. In the middle of the village, Castle Street
branches off, and it is possible to park on a side street. Return
to Castle Street, walk back to the A541, turn left and the signed
footpath is on the other side of the road. A panel advertises a
20-minute walk to the castle (no other route is available), but
this septuagenarian climbed to the castle through a pleasant
wood in ten minutes.

• **History** Caergwrle's history was brief but rather special,
since it is one of the last native Welsh castles, paradoxically
built with English money by English craftsmen. Dafydd ap
Gruffudd had betrayed his brother Llywelyn ap Gruffudd in
1274 to join with Edward I. He contributed 200 soldiers to
Edward's swift campaign of 1276–77 which forced Llywelyn's
surrender. Edward rewarded Dafydd with the *cantrefi* or
lordships of Rhufoniog and Dyffryn Clwyd, which included
strongholds at Hope and Denbigh. He furthermore contributed
one hundred marks (1 mark = 13s.4d., therefore £66 13s.4d.)
towards the building by Dafydd of a new castle at Caergwrle.

It is impossible to know whether the castle was complete
when Dafydd staged a sensational revolt against Edward at
Easter 1282. He claimed that Edward had not kept all the
promises made to him, but Edward not surprisingly was

The ragged wreck of Caergwrle.

outraged. The rebellion began with the storming of Hawarden castle and the capture of its lord, Roger de Clifford, and was followed by the taking of Dinas Brân and the new castle at Ruthin. By the time that Llywelyn had placed himself at the head of the rebellion and Edward began his retaliation, if not before, Dafydd deliberately wrecked Caergwrle and filled the well with stones. The king seized the site, repaired it (DJC King suggests that it was largely rebuilt) and put it in the care of Queen Eleanor, but a fire destroyed all the timber buildings in the inner ward and the site was abandoned.

• **Buildings** The *caer-* of the place-name suggests there may have been an Iron Age fort on this summit, though it awaits proof. The steep drop on the south and west sides made the task of building defences easy enough in those directions. On the north and east the curtain walls are defended by ditches and banks. Although rectangular, the castle only had two towers (roughly NE and SE) while the third tower was the keep, all in Gwespyr sandstone. The north-east tower is a typically Welsh D-shaped plan. It is impossible to know how much of the remaining fabric is pre-1282. Although badly ruined, the castle retains many features for the keen-eyed to spot; there is an oven by the south-east tower, latrines can be seen on the outside of the north-east tower, and at least one fireplace still remains.

EWLOE

SJ 288 675. Open access.

• **Access** Ewloe Castle is **not** in Ewloe village; the castle lies north of the A494, the village to the south. Do not be put off by the almost complete lack of signs. Inadequate signs exist for Wepre Country Park where the castle lies, and it can be reached from two directions. The shorter walk is from a lay-by on the B5125 between Ewloe and Northop Hall. The footpath leads north-eastwards across a large pasture towards a thick wood which hides the castle. The longer walk (some 15 minutes) leads westwards through the wood from the Wepre Park visitor centre, where leaflets are available. Wepre Park is signed both from the Mold Road and the main road between Connahs Quay and Shotton. Access to both park and castle is free. Cadw have published an excellent guide jointly for Ewloe and nearby Flint. Not suitable for wheelchair users.

• **History** The castle is splendidly perched on a steep-sided promontory looking eastward. It is now surrounded by fine trees, but that can hardly have been the case in the thirteenth century, though admittedly it was described in 1311 as being 'in the corner of a wood'. Much clearing would have taken place not only to provide timber for building but to give good views, especially eastwards over roads from Chester.

Llywelyn ap Gruffudd had taken advantage of the chaos in

Ewloe, Llywelyn ap Gruffudd's forest haunt.

England in the mid-1250s to break out from his Snowdonia heartland eastwards to the Dee, reclaiming lands controlled by his grandfather Llywelyn the Great. He began Ewloe Castle in 1257 and held it until the first invasion by Edward I in 1277, when the royal army swept the Welsh frontier back to the river Conwy. Ewloe Castle is not heard of again in either of the revolts of 1282–83 and 1294.

• **Buildings** The castle site was already secured on three sides by steep slopes, so Llywelyn ordered a massive ditch to be cut east–west across the promontory to protect it from the south. On the south side of this ditch there is a large earth rampart whose purpose is uncertain. Attackers from that direction already had a good vantage point from which to pour fire into the castle. Was the rampart put there to force them to expose themselves to the defenders' fire, or is it part of a putative English siege-work of around 1277. Certainly it is not simply spoil from the ditch; the easy way to dispose of that would be simply to shift it sideways and down the slopes. If the castle was garrisoned during Llywelyn's rule, as seems likely, then there must have been some local development to provide accommodation for men and women servicing the castle, like the little settlement outside Castell y Bere, but none is visible in the woods.

The castle itself, built of local Holling rock, is irregular in plan, fitted between the ditch and the natural slopes. It is divided into two wards, upper and lower. The upper ward contains the massive remains of what is known as the Welsh tower, and indeed it is of the D-shape common to a number of other Welsh castles. The climb up this tower to the present viewing platform gives a splendid overview of the castle plan, though it should be remembered that the castle was originally higher than it is now. The principal room of the tower would have been at first-floor level, above a basement probably used for storage and accessed by trap-door and ladder. The curtain walls of both wards have been so degraded that it is not easy to imagine the wall-walk which extended to the west tower, the lower part of which is built against the living rock.

FLINT

SJ 247 733. Cadw. Open access in daylight hours.

• **Access**   Flint Castle, like Ewloe, is not easily found, but repays the effort; the ruins are much more accessible and better cared for than they were in the 1960s, when the old Flint jail stood alongside and the surroundings were generally less salubrious than they are now. The town itself is a puzzle for unfamiliar drivers, especially if approached from Ewloe, and the only sign on the main street is for pedestrians, not motorists. The A548 runs from Chester through the town towards Holywell closely parallel to the railway, which has to be crossed just south-east of the station by a humped bridge; then the castle comes into view, right on the Dee estuary. Drive right round the front of the castle to the car park. Admission is free, but the gate to the castle is locked nightly. Cadw publishes an excellent guide jointly with Ewloe, but it cannot be bought at the site.

• **History**   Flint is one of Edward's first series of castles (with Builth, Rhuddlan, Denbigh and Aberystwyth), all designed as a power statement containing the shrunken rump of Gwynedd which Llywelyn ap Gruffudd was allowed to retain after his 1277 surrender. The choice of site may seem a puzzle, since today it languishes almost at sea-level, immediately above a great stretch of marsh and cut off by the railway from the town. Edward used Flint to fill a gap between Chester and the new fortress he intended for Rhuddlan; each of the three places being a day's march apart along the level, mostly coastal

Flint, Earliest of Edward I's North Wales castles.

route. This was a wiser plan than attempting to penetrate the forests and valleys of the Welsh interior. Ewloe had almost certainly been taken from the Welsh, but it would have been useless for Edward's purposes. Moreover Flint could at the time be reached easily by boat, making it possible to supply the castle from Chester in the event of a siege.

It took Edward's men ten days to clear the route from Chester to Flint, where a temporary base with a timber palisade was established in July 1277. The following month it was at Flint that Llywelyn's renegade brother Dafydd, who had deserted to Edward in 1274, made a compact with Edward by which he would be rewarded for his support of the Crown with lands conquered from Llywelyn. While Edward moved on towards Rhuddlan, by the end of August nearly three thousand men were employed in preparing the new castle and its walled borough. The first task was to dig a massive ditch round castle and town; by 1278 quarrymen were cutting stone on the Wirral to be ferried across the Dee and in 1280 a limekiln was constructed to aid the building work. By November Master James of St George, Edward's architectural genius, was being paid to supervise and no doubt develop the design work.

The castle was still incomplete at Easter 1282 when the twice-treacherous Dafydd rose in revolt against the Crown. His army captured Hawarden and burnt the new borough of Flint but failed to capture the castle. Just over a year later Dafydd's own men betrayed him to Edward, and he was hanged, drawn and quartered at Shrewsbury. In the meantime the building and reconstruction work at Flint castle and town continued. It was largely complete when in 1294 the Welsh rose in rebellion under Madog ap Llywelyn. This time the castle's constable burnt the town to deny it to the rebels, and the castle held out successfully against the subsequent Welsh siege.

Edward's great Statute of Wales in 1284 created the county of Flintshire, with the new town as its administrative centre, subordinate to Chester. The castle was maintained in good order for the rest of the medieval period, and was the scene of Richard II's surrender to Henry Bolingbroke in August 1399. It played its last rôle in history during the Civil Wars. Royalist forces lost and regained it in 1643, lost and regained it again in 1645 and finally lost it to the victorious parliamentarians in 1646. It was ordered to be slighted, and by 1652 it was a ruin, though much has survived. The burgesses of Flint no doubt carried much stone away for their own building purposes.

• **Buildings** The castle plan is not symmetrical, though the inner ward, with its massive walls of Wirral sandstone partly surviving, is almost square. The foundation walls in the yard represent much later medieval buildings. Three of the corner towers are similar in size, but the south-west one is known as the Great Tower on account of its massive dimensions. It is protected by a ditch and was accessible via a small bridge, so that in the unlikely event of an enemy breaking into the inner ward the garrison could retreat into the Tower. This is the most unusual feature of the castle, anticipating by more than a century the (even larger) Yellow Tower of Gwent at Raglan; both are castles within castles. The walls at the base are seven metres thick. Moreover, there is effectively a tower within the Great Tower. At basement level a stone-vaulted gallery runs round between the inner and outer towers; at first floor level, where the outer tower wall is thinner, a series of rooms runs round the building, their dividing walls pointing inwards like spokes. Unfortunately the modern gate to the Great Tower is now kept padlocked because it became a resort of winos, and visitors can no longer appreciate this remarkable building.

HAWARDEN

SJ 319 654. Private; occasional opening.

• **Access** This is the only castle described in this book which I have failed to visit, but not for want of effort. It is privately owned by the Gladstone family, who open the park on occasional Sundays. I chose the wrong Sunday (there seems no easy way of finding out which are the right ones, nor is the castle visible from public land or footpath). The castle's gates are on the crossroads in the middle of Hawarden village south of Queensferry, with dates of opening posted, but the entrance is on the east side of the village. The account below is based on other authorities.

• **History** A motte survives near Hawarden church; a second was in existence by 1205, when it was attacked by the Welsh. This was the home of the Monthaut family, but by 1264 it was under the aegis of Simon de Montfort, who for a few months

The closed gates of Hawarden castle.

was virtual ruler of England, with Henry III his captive. It was here in 1264 that Simon allied himself with Llywelyn ap Gruffudd, granted him the castle and promised him his daughter Eleanor's hand in marriage, but with Simon's death the following August Llywelyn had to seize the castle by main force; however in 1267 he returned it to Monthaut family control. By 1282 it was in the charge of Roger Clifford. On 21 March, Llywelyn's brother Dafydd ap Gruffudd, who had assisted Edward I in the war of 1277, swooped on Hawarden at night, seizing the castle, and thus began the Welsh revolt which ended with the deaths of the two Welsh princes. Work may have begun in stone before the Welsh attack; it was completed, and the castle successfully defended over a century later against Glyndŵr's rebels. In the Civil War it withstood ten months of parliamentarian siege before surrendering in March 1646, and subsequently became a landscape feature in the Gladstone family estate, of which it is still a part.

• **Buildings** The castle's finest feature is a splendid round tower not unlike that at Flint, but having a mural passage at first-floor level rather than the ground floor, and there is a chapel inside the wall. The curtain walls are ruinous, though one part is high enough to have retained the window openings which would have lit the great hall. Apart from the keep there appears only to have been one other tower, whose base survives.

RHUDDLAN

SJ 024 779. Cadw. Fee.

• **Access** Compared with the other Flintshire castles described in this chapter, Rhuddlan is easy to find. Coming along the A55 from the west, take the left turn for Rhyl and Rhuddlan; coming from the east, take the turn for St Asaph, pass through the little city to the bottom of the hill and turn right towards Rhyl and Rhuddlan. The road leads to a four-way roundabout; take the third exit (A525) towards Rhuddlan; the castle is soon visible across the river Clwyd. Turn right over the river and at the top of the the the slope turn right into Castle Street. There is a car park, Cadw ticket office and visitors' centre.

• **History**   Rhuddlan is arguably the oldest continuously-occupied urban site in Wales. English invaders won a famous victory over the Welsh in the vicinity in 796; in 921 they established a fortified borough here, but the Welsh had reoccupied it by 1050. When the Normans swept into north Wales their leader established a motte-and-bailey castle in 1073, with a new borough, and he became known as Robert of Rhuddlan. Eventually the Welsh regained it in about 1150 and held it, with two intervals, until 1277. The castle mound, known as Twthill, is only a few minutes' walk from the car park.

The lowest bridging point on the Clwyd for centuries was at Rhuddlan, and the position was therefore strategically important. In August 1277 Edward I, on reaching the river in his drive against Llywelyn ap Gruffudd, decided on a new situation for his intended castle with a new borough, and ditch-diggers from Flint began work not only on the site but

*Rhuddlan: Edward's message of menace to the Welsh,
victim of later stone-robbers.*

on deepening the Clwyd so that sea-access would be possible
from the harbour they created beside the castle. Early in 1278
James of St George, the master-builder whom Edward had
encountered on the Continent, arrived at Rhuddlan to take
charge of his first commission for the king. By 1282, when
over £9,000 had been spent, the castle was able to withstand
the onslaught of the great Welsh revolt of that year, though not
without damage, and Edward made it his headquarters for his
successful war of 1282–83. With the end of hostilities, it was
at Rhuddlan in 1284 that Edward promulgated his Statute of
Wales, which laid down the administration of the country for
250 years, and he offered a thousand marks (£666 13s.4d.)

towards moving the diocesan cathedral from St Asaph to his new borough.

Rhuddlan remained a royal castle in good condition after the Welsh wars, since Flintshire was royal territory, administered from Chester. It withstood Glyndŵr's attacks in 1400 and 1405, and was still defensible when occupied by the royal army in the Civil War, until Major-General Thomas Mytton's successful siege of 1646, after which the castle was deliberately made untenable. The authorities were certainly helped in this by the burgesses of the borough seeing their chance to strip the best reachable stone for rebuilding their houses, as is clear all the way round the outside of the towers and curtain walls.

• **Buildings** The castle's plan repays investigation by the visitor. The present access is close to the site of the original Town Gate. The dry moat runs leftwards around the outer ward to the Friary Gate (blocked in 1300); some of its impressive stone revetting is still in place. On the right the ground slopes down towards the river Clwyd, originally defended with a wall and two corner towers. At the far end of the wall is Gillot's tower, protecting the dock gate, and it was here that ships were once able to put in to unload. All the principal masonry is of carboniferous limestone.

The inner castle is still massively impressive, especially the giant twin entrance towers at the east and west corners, each four stories high. The SE and SW curtain walls are unbroken, but the two opposite walls were badly slighted in the seventeenth century. The ruins may seem bleak and unwelcome now, but in their royal heyday, with all the additional accommodation for people (and horses) available in timber buildings, the castle would have been full of colour and activity, with a good deal of comfort for the most privileged occupants and visitors. Rhuddlan remains one of the great castles of Wales.

GLAMORGAN

CAERPHILLY – *CAERFFILI*

ST 156 871. Cadw. Fee.

• **Access**   Although Caerphilly's comparatively low-lying position does not allow it to dominate its urban setting as do Caernarfon, Harlech and Conway theirs, nevertheless it is a giant castle even on a European scale of castle-building, right in the town centre; once the visitor enters, the town simply fades away – the fortifications are all. This is said to be the second largest castle in the United Kingdom (one authority says 'after Windsor', another claims 'after Dover'). The only deterrent to visitors is the shortage of parking; there is a small car park close to the castle, which is usable on Sundays and Bank Holidays, or there is a larger one some minutes' walk away. Demonstrations of medieval siege artillery and re-enactments of medieval life are a regular feature of castle activities. Excellent guidebook.

• **History**   Why so huge? It is only by grasping a little history that the question can be answered. In the early 1260s the upland Welsh lordship of Senghennydd was sandwiched between the lowland Glamorgan lordship of the de Clares and the lordship of Brecon, newly seized by Llywelyn ap Gruffudd of Gwynedd. Gilbert de Clare, young, hugely wealthy and energetic, was determined to take over the Welsh uplands while Llywelyn, ambitious and successful in war, wanted their lords' allegiance to extend his principality. Conflict was inevitable; both men were formidable characters. Gilbert seized the lordship of Senghennydd and began building the castle here in 1268. Llywelyn attacked and burnt it in 1270.

Henry III persuaded the Welsh prince to hold off, putting the castle in the hands of two English bishops, but they turned a blind eye when Gilbert's friends took possession. By 1272 the building was largely completed, and Llywelyn did not attack again. Later the castle resisted the Welsh uprisings of 1295 and 1316; in 1326 Edward II was briefly here in the last dreadful months of his reign, and the castle was besieged by his enemies for months. Thereafter it declined rapidly; Owain Glyndŵr is not recorded to have attacked it, and by 1539 it was a colossal ruin. It played no known part in the Civil Wars, although the ramparts opposite the west island date from that period.

Activity recommenced on the site in 1928, when its owner the fourth marquess of Bute, son of the recreator of Cardiff and Castell Coch, mounted a sober restoration of the inner ward and battlements, and splendidly remade the Great Hall, as well as pulling down houses which had been built against the outer walls. When it passed to the Ministry of Works in 1950 the lakes were re-flooded and the site transformed.

• **Buildings** Even more than its huge walls of Pennant sandstone, what is most impressive is the extent of water which defends the site. No other castle in Wales has anything like it; Gilbert may have adopted the idea from Kenilworth castle, which he would have visited. Indeed he may even have chosen the Caerphilly site because it could be conveniently flooded. His unknown architect was certainly conversant with the latest ideas in castle planning.

The water features are on two levels. The visitor approaches by crossing the southern and lower strip of water or partial moat to the main Gatehouse, which survives fairly complete because it was long used as the local prison. The great embankment on which the gatehouse stands actually holds back the upper twin lakes. Turning left from the ticket office,

Gilbert de Clare's splendid Caerphilly Castle. Crown copyright RCAHMW.

pass the ruined corn-mill whose wheel was driven for four centuries by the flow from the upper lakes to the moat. Thus reach the south dam, on which are mounted the reconstructed siege-engines. The turrets set against the dam-wall have been torn away by ground subsidence.

Return to the gatehouse and pass through a passageway onto the north dam. After walking along this, return towards the passageway and turn right onto the north bank which partially divides the north and south lakes. In the summer scores of sandmartins rush to and fro across the north lake before returning to their nests in the castle wall; anglers wait expectantly for the coarse fish with which the lake is stocked. The north bank reaches right round to the western island, by which a drawbridge reached to the main castle; the entrance is usually closed. From the north bank look across the water to the Civil War ramparts, located on top of a no-longer-visible Roman fort.

Returning to the Gatehouse, the visitor should enjoy the exhibitions in the galleries before approaching the East Gate, crossing water for the second time. Prior to entering the gate, turn left to examine the famous leaning tower, whose incline is due to ground subsidence. The frontage of the huge East Gate has been largely rebuilt, but the inward facing wall is still complete. The building contained a whole suite of domestic buildings, making it a keep as well as a gatehouse; the interior is not open to visitors.

Looking from the East Gate across the inner ward to the West Gate, on the left is the Great Hall, a fourteenth-century addition to the main structure, restored by the fourth Marquess of Bute, and containing refreshment facilities. To the left of the hall was a building containing a buttery and pantry at ground level, with a chapel above. To the right of the hall was a complex of domestic apartments. Opposite the hall, a fighting platform has been reconstructed of the kind which would enable defenders to shoot at any besieging force.

Visitors to the inner ward will realise that this is the heart of the castle. Surrounded mostly by buildings, the whole is protected by middle wards, themselves defended by water, which made undermining works impossible. The only points of access, the original double drawbridges to west and east, are both well defended by overlooking towers, and even had an enemy penetrated to the middle wards, the heart of the castle was still secured by massive walls and gates. Caerffili was the work of a man who did not hesitate to defy even Edward I when he saw fit; Gilbert's arrogance speaks from the stones.

CARDIFF

ST 180 767. Open all year. Fee.

• **Access** Cardiff's municipally-owned castle is so splendid and so central that it is hard to miss. Parking is the problem; central multi-storey car parks are not cheap, but bus and train access to the city are convenient. It must be admitted that these expenses, added to the admission fees, make a visit to Cardiff castle a costly experience; on the other hand, this is one of the greatest historic building complexes in Britain, a must-be-seen. The temporary access offices outside the main gate are to be replaced by a permanent centre inside the gate on the right. Visitors may choose to visit only the grounds, medieval keep and Military Museum, or they may pay more for guided tours of the later buildings and the Bute Tower. The Military Museum is well worth a visit, not least for the exhibit devoted to family life and the rôle of women in an apparently all-male world of guns and medals.

• **History and Buildings** The high battlemented walls which surround three sides of the castle are a Victorian rebuild of an original Roman fort, whose foundations can still be seen in many places both within and without. As a re-creation its only serious fault is that the Romans did not usually build their forts with such high walls. In fact four different Roman structures occupied the site between AD 80 and 400; what we see recreated here is the last, a fourth century eight-acre fort with walls ten feet thick. An entire community lived within, and communicated by road and sea with other Roman towns and ports.

As in a number of other places (see e.g. Tomen-y-mur, Merionethshire) the Normans chose a Roman site for their first castle on the river Taf; the nature of the site and the huge supply of stone made the choice an easy one. They created the giant moated mound near the site-centre for their first timber castle. The present twelve-sided limestone keep was built about 1140 (its gatehouse is a fifteenth-century addition). A notable prisoner in the tower was Robert, duke of Normandy, elder brother of Henry I, imprisoned there for years by royal command. The most famous incident in its history was the successful raid by Ifor Bach, Welsh lord of Senghennydd, who stormed the keep in 1158 and captured his overlord, Earl William of Glamorgan, and carried him and his family into the hills. Ifor's name is still popularly recognised in the culture of this part of Wales. A century later the threat of Llywelyn ap Gruffudd was such that Gilbert de Clare (see Caerphilly) built the Black Tower (now housing the Military Museum) at the ruined Roman south gate, and linked it to the keep by a massive wall whose foundations survive.

With Gilbert de Clare's death in 1314 without an heir, Cardiff passed into royal custody, and Gilbert's Welsh friend and ally Llywelyn Bren, the cultured great-grandson of Ifor Bach, protested against the brutal administration of the royal appointee Pain de Turberville of Coety. Following the failure

Cardiff's western range, sixteenth–nineteenth century.

of his appeal to Edward II, Llywelyn raised revolt in south-east Wales in 1316 which was quickly overcome, and he surrendered to avoid further suffering by his people, and next year was treacherously and brutally executed by Turberville's successor, the monstrous Hugh le Despenser.

In 1403 the Glyndŵr revolt reached Cardiff; town and castle were fiercely besieged and much damage done; substantial relief only reached the garrison from Devon a year later. Thereafter peace descended on south-east Wales; in the 1420s the new owner of the castle, Richard Beauchamp, earl of Warwick, began building accommodation on the castle's west wall; the Octagon tower dates from this period. By the late sixteenth century those virtual owners of Cardiff the Herbert family, later earls of Pembroke, held the castle and improved the recent buildings to a high level of luxury for the age; there is a good Herbert tomb in the fine church of St John nearby, open in daylight hours. The fourth earl sided with Parliament against Charles I, who confiscated his lands, but the family eventually regained them. Lands and castle passed by marriage first to Thomas, viscount Windsor (1704), and in 1766 to Lord Mountstuart, Earl and future first marquess of Bute.

The site was transformed; Capability Brown cleared most of the castle green, filled in the moat (later restored in part) and planted fine trees. Henry Holland transformed the west buildings, rebuilding the north wing and adding one to the south; all can still be seen from the Green. This work proceeded by fits and starts between 1770 and 1814, when the second Marquess of Bute began the transformation of Cardiff by creating its docks for the export of coal, especially from mines on his own lands, thus making himself enormously rich. He spent much more time at the castle than did his forebears, but it was his son, the third Marquess (1847–1900), who really made the castle what it is today, re-excavating the moat and beginning the restoration of the Roman fort.

In 1865 the teenage Marquess met and began a famous collaboration with William Burges, an architect-designer in love with medieval Gothic. There followed the building of the clock tower at the castle's SW corner. The Marquess loved towers; those existing were heightened and others added. Buildings were gutted so that larger rooms could be built, especially the great banqueting hall. Any first-time visitor who has not seen the other major Bute–Burges creation at Castell Coch will be overwhelmed by the extraordinary richness and complexity of the decoration in every room. It involved stonework, sculpture, mosaic, marquetry, tiles, candelabra, carpentry, stained glass, furniture and wallcoverings of the highest quality. All is a riot of birds, butterflies, monkeys, medieval literature, biblical and

Arabic legend, touches of astrology, with a nursery which is a colourful riot of children's tales and nursery rhymes.

The clock tower was envisaged as a chaste male retreat of smoking rooms and a bachelor bedroom, guarded by a vivid ceiling-devil. The bachelor's bath is a remodelled Roman sarcophagus imported from Italy. The nursery is in the guest tower; tours continue via the extraordinary Arab room (a fantasy harem), the Chaucer room (Lady Bute's sitting room), Lord Bute's bedroom and the roof garden in the Bute tower, the small dining room, the library (now disappointingly almost devoid of books), the chapel and the wonderful banqueting hall. The serious visitor will have only one regret – that the tour is over too quickly to take in so much amazing detail.

CASTELL COCH

ST 131 826. Cadw. Fee.

• **Access**   This is one of the most popular of the smaller Welsh stone castles. Its extensive carpark is easily accessed via Tongwynlais from the A470 dual carriageway between Cardiff and Merthyr Tudful. Springtime visitors will quickly become aware of the swathes of ramsons (wild garlic) flowering in the extensive woodlands, and at any time of year can enjoy walking there. There is an excellent tearoom in the castle.

• **History**   Castell Coch is unique, a Welsh castle whose massive medieval foundations support a Victorian pseudomedieval fantasy beloved of filmmakers, the creation of the Victorian architect-designer William Burges and his patron, that plutocratic dreamer the third Marquess of Bute. The original castle was clearly Welsh in origin, and was splendidly sited to guard the southern entrance to the Taf gorge. It is situated in the Welsh lordship of Senghennydd, which retained

Castell Coch. Crown copyright RCAHMW.

considerable independence until 1266, by which time there was certainly a castle on the site, perhaps the work of the last Welsh lord, Gruffudd ap Rhys. He was imprisoned by Gilbert de Clare, Lord of Glamorgan and creator of Caerphilly castle. Gilbert certainly remodelled and possibly rebuilt much of the castle whose ruins were photographed before the Bute-Burges recreation. There are no records of any part it may have played in medieval history.

• **Buildings** Before entering, the visitor should look at the external foundations. The gatehouse and its flanking towers are Victorian rebuilds, but following round to the left, one is looking at medieval red (hence the title *coch* = red) sandstone work, comprising the base of the hall, the keep and much of the curtain wall at the rear. The towers are surprisingly large considering the diminutive size of the castle yard. Inside, Burges and his successors created a reasonable facsimile of a medieval courtyard, but walk into the hall buildings on the left and the vision becomes fantasy, a riot of decorative sculpture, painting, mosaic and tiles, not to mention some impressive furniture.

COETY

SS 923 816. Cadw. Open access. daylight.

• **Access** Coety means 'house in the wood'; the form Coity is common on maps and signposts. These fine and complex ruins are on a low ridge overlooking much of the Vale of Glamorgan. To reach them, leave the M4 at junction 36, following the A4061 (signs for Bridgend) for almost a kilometre, then left at roundabout (signs for Coety). In Coety village turn left and immediately right into castle car park. There is an excellent Cadw guidebook for Coety, Ogmore and Newcastle (Bridgend) jointly, though since none of the three has a visitor centre, it

Coety Castle, Bridgend.

must be bought elsewhere or ordered. Coety stands next to a large medieval church with tomb effigies of two of the castle's medieval family members.

• **History**   Coety's original ringwork of bank and ditch, which is still reflected in the castle's plan, dates from the conquest of Glamorgan between the Taf and Ogmore rivers by Robert Fitzhamon (d.1107), following the death of Rhys ap Tewdwr in 1093. Robert's follower Pain de Turberville built the ringwork; his grandson Gilbert built the curtain walls and keep before 1200. The same family kept Coety for another 150 years. Another Gilbert de Turberville (d.1349) built the outer ward and extensively remodelled the earlier buildings to a high standard, so that his grandson and successor Sir Lawrence Berkerolles was able to welcome Richard II and his court in 1394.

The castle had probably seen no military action before the long Glyndŵr siege of 1404–05, when the castle had to be relieved twice, by Henry, Prince of Wales and by his father Henry IV, at great expense. The castle was much damaged, but put into repair, and the chapel completed. By this time the wealthy Gamage family had succeeded by marriage to ownership of the castle. The Gamages did not endure; the heiress Barbara (d.1621) married Robert Sidney, Earl of Leicester (d. 1626), brother of Sir Philip Sidney, and Coety remained in Sidney hands for a century as a subsidiary home before passing to the Earl of Dunraven in 1833, after which it was vacated and fell into ruin.

• **Buildings** Entering the outer ward at the west end through the remains of the fifteenth-century gatehouse, the visitor sees on the right the remains of an enormous fifteenth-century barn, a feature also found at Llansteffan, and beyond it the remains of the south gatehouse. Through the fourteenth-century middle gatehouse is the inner ward, surrounded by an almost circular twelfth century wall, founded on the original ringwork bank. The three-storey keep of the same period is on the left, and beyond it stands the fine fifteenth-century NE gatehouse. Opposite the middle gatehouse is the chapel, then comes the undercroft of the main hall with a latrine tower beyond. The service range lies between the hall and the middle gatehouse. The supports of what must have been fine vaulted roofs survive in the keep and hall. All the masonry is of local Querella limestone. In the ward are the foundations of a large building whose function is unknown. It makes better sense of the ruins to realise that much of castle life was lived on the first storey level, not ground level.

FONMON

ST 047 681. Private home; see below.

• **Access** West of Barry the A4226 becomes the B4206, and two signed southward turnings lead one to Fonmon village, where the estate gates lead to a small car park. Although still a private home, Fonmon Castle is open to visitors on Tuesday and Wednesday afternoons between 1 April and 30 September. A guide leads tours at 2, 3 and 4 p.m. Other visits can be arranged by appointment: 01446 710206. The fee is expensive but well worth while. The gardens are delightful.

• **History and Buildings** The manor of Fonmon was the property of Oliver St John, who *c*.1200 chose a fine site for his castle high above the Thaw river; it was considerably extended in the thirteenth century. The castle seems never to have been

Fonmon Castle: the medieval keep is centre-right.

attacked, and in 1656 was sold by the St John family to Colonel Philip Jones, the most prominent south Wales figure in the Cromwellian commonwealth and controller of the dictator's household. In the eighteenth century it was again extended to form a small mansion of austere appearance, now much softened by Virginia creeper. The keep is still central to the frontal composition, but the entrance is on the right to a small nineteenth-century office. The finest rooms are the splendid hall with family and royal portraits, and the magnificent upstairs library.

GOWER'S CASTLES

• **Access**   A sunny weekday in Gower is close to heaven; weekends are too crowded. There are splendid beaches and moorland walking, with castles to boot. The Normans took over the Welsh *cantref* of Gower as a lordship which reached from Kilvay to Worm's Head and from Mumbles to Pontardawe. Strictly speaking Swansea and Oystermouth castles were the main Gower castles and are dealt with individually. Despite Llywelyn the Great's seizure of the lordship in 1217, the peninsula's castles experienced little warfare and three are better described as fortified manor houses, a class largely omitted from this book. They can be found as follows:

Pennard *SS 544 855. Cadw.* The castle is nearly two miles beyond the village, perched on a cliff edge but vulnerable to sand accumulation. Park near the golf club and walk with care on the public footpath across the golf course. The carboniferous limestone gatehouse and fine curtain wall are late thirteenth/ early fourteenth century.

Weobley's simple entrance and pleasant courtyard.

Oxwich *SS 498 863. Cadw. Fee.* Follow the A4118 from Killay through Nicholaston; a mile later follow the signs left to Oxwich and the 'castle', really an impressive Tudor manor house.

Penrice *SS 497 885. Private land; public footpath close by.* As for Oxwich but take the following left turn down a very narrow road. A small parking place gives access by public footpath to view but not visit the site of this small neglected thirteenth-century castle.

Weobley *SS 478 928. Cadw. Fee.* Two miles west of Llanrhidian village turn right for the limited parking space. This is the finest castle site in Gower, perched on a bluff overlooking the broad Loughor estuary, Llanrhidian sandmarshes and Llanelli, well worth a visit for the views alone. Tickets are available at the farmhouse close by. Although the outer walls of carboniferous limestone look forbidding, the entrance lacks the usual array of defence mechanisms. The towers were useful for accommodation and toilet provision rather than warfare. The south-west tower is the oldest surviving part (thirteenth century). The east block was remodelled in the fifteenth century, with a limekiln beyond. The fine hall on the north side had a kitchen at ground level. To the west is the solar, with cellars below, which would once have been a comfortable room.

LOUGHOR

SS 564 980. Open access.

• **Access** The A484 from Swansea to Llanelli crosses the river Loughor immediately after the roundabout where it is joined by the A4240. Turn off the A484 at the roundabout and keep left down to the free riverside car park. Walk up Ferry Road

The last stump of Loughor Castle.

and the castle mound rises before you the other side of the A4240. It may not be a castle worth travelling to see, but it is worth a visit if you are in the locality, and there is a pleasant pub opposite.

• History and Building This small but once solid castle stood guard over an important crossing-point of the Loughor, which though not prominent among Welsh rivers, has long been a major political boundary between the lordships of Kidwelly and Gower, then between Glamorgan and Carmarthenshire. The Romans built a fort at this river crossing-point, Leucarium, of which Henry de Villiers took advantage in the early twelfth century, creating a ringwork on a motte-like mound. This was burnt by the Welsh in 1151. It passed with the lordship of Gower into the possession of the de Braose family, who constructed the stone castle of which the remaining tower was once part. Fireplaces, windows and the garderobe are still clearly to be seen, suggesting a place of some comfort, however dilapidated it has since become. It played no known part in Welsh history after the mid-thirteenth century.

MORLAIS

SO 048 097 Open access.

• **Access** Finding Morlais is half the battle, but one worth fighting. There are no signposts or Cadw plaques of any kind, and most of the existing guidebooks are either silent or seriously vague on how to get there. Having got there, one is bound to sympathise with their problem. Best perhaps to approach on

Morlais castle. Crown copyright RCAHMW.

the Heads of the Valleys road (A465). Two kilometres west of the Dowlais Top roundabout, three kilometres east of the junction with the Cardiff–Brecon dual carriageway (A487) there are slip roads which will lead one to the village of Pant. If coming from the east, run up to the Galon Uchaf roundabout and cross the bridge over the A465. If coming from the west, leave the A465 and turn sharp left. These two roads meet; follow signs for the Brecon Mountain Railway, keeping left at the cemetery. Shortly one reaches the entrance to the Morlais Castle Golf Club, on the left just before the railway station on the right. I found the club staff very willing for castle visitors to use their car park, and most helpful with directions. Take the path past No 1 tee, and after a hundred yards bear left cautiously across the fairway and along a track in the rough. Reach the top of the gentle slope, and the castle fills the view. Bear left towards the castle's ragged entrance, and there is a simple stile over the fence. Beware other instructions; parking at the golf club is safe and the path easy. Views over this green, rocky, once-industrial landscape are splendid. Some visitors may find the site wreckage repulsive; I found it fascinating.

• **History**   This site at 370 metres above sea level, where one might have expected a Welsh prince rather than a Norman lord to build, is one of the most unusual in Wales. The land here was claimed by Humphrey de Bohun, Lord of Brecon, but coveted by Gilbert de Clare, Lord of Glamorgan and builder of Caerphilly with money loaned by Florentine bankers. About the year 1288 Gilbert took possession of the great limestone ridge (already occupied by a substantial Iron Age hill fort); had his men cut a massive trench across the ridge, cutting off the southern part of the fort, and build walls on the rest of the hillfort's ramparts and raise massive towers. At least there was plentiful limestone all around. In 1290, war flared up between the two turkey-cock marcher lords, and Edward summoned the miscreants before him, fining both of them for breaking the peace. Gilbert's efforts were in vain; during the brief but ferocious Welsh rebellion of 1294, the castle was stormed and destroyed by the local leader, Morgan ap Maredudd, and his men, who also captured Llantrisant, Kenfig and Llangynwyd castles. Edward briefly visited the site on his post-revolt tour of Wales in summer 1295; Morlais was never to be rebuilt.

• **Buildings** With a single exception, the site is completely shattered, but none the less highly intriguing. One enters the wrecked south-east doorway to reach the outer court. The most striking feature is the giant cistern, 14 metres deep and roughly 7 by 7 metres across, and so steeply cut that anyone who fell in would, even if not injured, need the skills of a serious rock-climber to escape. Beyond the cistern a wall-footing divides the outer from the inner ward, and within are the foundations of the hall. Returning to the entrance (avoiding the western rampart, sheer above a quarry floor), there is the mighty south keep, looking rather like a motte. However, it reveals a special feature; a vaulted chamber with twelve supporting arches springing from a single column, rather like a cathedral chapter-house, restored by Cadw.

NEWCASTLE (Bridgend)

SS902801. Usually open (free) 10–4.

• **Access** This little-known castle stands on a steep escarpment looking east over the river Ogmore and Bridgend, next to St Illtyd's church. From Bridgend take the A473 westwards up Park Street, signed for Laleston. First right (St Leonard's Road), right at T-junction with West Street, drive to end, where there is a small car park.

*The fine gateway
at Newcastle Bridgend.*

• **History** This is one of the triangle of castles (with Coety and Ogmore) marking the westward thrust of Robert Fitzhamon across Glamorgan after 1093, built as a ringwork by his follower William de Londres. It was strengthened in stone later in the twelfth century and a central keep built, which has disappeared. The Londres family held it for several generations. The death in 1183 of Earl William of Gloucester, lord of Glamorgan, gave the Welsh a chance to rebel, and Henry II took the lordship into his own hands, marrying his son John to Isabella, Earl William's daughter. John therefore became lord of Glamorgan on Henry's death, and most remarkably he ceded tenure of Newcastle to Morgan ap Caradog, leader of the 1183 rebellion, for some years. In 1217 it was granted to the Turbervilles of Coety and used as a dwelling for many years. Glyndŵr's rebellion seems to have passed it by, and it fell into ruin.

• **Buildings** Newcastle's buildings were little altered after 1200. Its finest feature is the splendid ornamented late Norman gateway, perhaps built during Henry II's tenure. Immediately to the left is the first of two massive square mural towers of the same period, of a kind soon replaced by semi-circular towers giving better control of the ground outside. The high curtain walls probably follow the line of the original ringwork. Whether there was an outer ward is unclear. The village outside has a distinctly older feel than the town of Bridgend, shattered by modern 'developers'.

OGMORE

SS 882 769. Cadw. Open access.

• **Access**   These attractive ruins, although more than a kilometre from the sea, stand only a little above sea level on the southern bank of the river Ewenny, just before it joins the Ogmore. They are best reached from the M4 by turning south-west on the A473. At the fourth roundabout turn left into the

Ogmore's riverside castle.

Ewenny road. Keep left onto the road for Ogmore-by-sea, and the castle ruins eventually become visible down on the right. A small turning leads to the little riverside car park, whence a fine line of stepping stones crosses the river from the castle to the opposite bank, which gives a good view of the ruins. Ogmore can be visited jointly with Ewenny's fortified priory, not always open, but interesting even from the outside.

• **History** Ogmore Castle, like Coety and Newcastle, was a ringwork established by William de Londres (d. before 1126), a follower of Robert Fitzhamon, as part of the latter's strengthening of his position in mid-Glamorgan before his death in 1107. A Welsh attack in 1116 forced William to abandon the site for a while, but the family soon resumed occupation; William's son Maurice (d.1149) was probably responsible for the stone keep; his splendid tomb lies in Ewenny priory church, founded by his father. Although the castle was the administrative centre of its own lordship of Ogmore, no large permanent settlement developed here; perhaps growth was inhibited by the marshy nature of the neighbourhood.

Maurice's grandsons, William and Thomas de Londres (d.1216) successively inherited Ogmore, and the latter's daughter took it by marriage in turn to three husbands, the last of whom, Patrick de Chaworth (d.1258), gave her a son, but his daughter married Henry, earl of Lancaster, and thus eventually Ogmore became a royal possession with the accession of Henry Bolingbroke. The castle suffered greatly at the hands of the Glyndŵr rebels, though whether it ever surrendered is not known. It was repaired, and a large building was established in the outer ward which remained a courthouse for the area until 1803; it is shown clearly in a painting by Paul Sandby (d.1809).

• **Buildings** The modern gate is on the site of the original gateway into the outer ward. The shell of the fifteenth-century courthouse is on the left. A modern bridge crosses the great ditch into the inner ward, occupying the interior of the original ringwork, whose circular banks were levelled when the curtain walls were built. The twelfth-century keep on the left would have been entered by a stairway up to the first floor level; a second floor and other alterations were added in the following century, including a latrine turret. Next to the keep are the foundations of what may have been the kitchen, followed by those of a large hall overlooking the river, added in the thirteenth century. This would have replaced the keep as the main centre of domestic life. The most intriguing feature of the ruins is the vaulted entrance to the 'cellar', probably used for storage. The foundations of a three-unit building lie close to the south curtain wall; its function is not clear.

OYSTERMOUTH

SS 613 883. Municipal. Fee.

• **Access** It is worth struggling with the Oystermouth traffic to visit this small but quite well-preserved and intriguing Marcher castle, with its fine views over Swansea Bay. Follow the A4067 from Swansea towards Mumbles and turn right uphill at the castle sign (B4593). Turn right into Castle Avenue for limited parking and the entrance. It can be combined with visits to the castles of Swansea and Gower. The castle is open daily for a small fee. The name 'Oystermouth' is a Norman corruption of the Welsh original, Ystum Llwynarth.

• **History** As part of the relentless Norman movement westwards, William de Londres of Ogmore established a ringwork here, only for it to be stormed by the Welsh in 1116. His son Maurice built a square stone keep which is at the heart of the present castle; this was stormed by the progeny of the Lord Rhys in 1215, but not retained by them. It passed to the de Braose lords of Gower, whose centre was Swansea Castle, but they seem to have preferred Oystermouth. It was attacked during Rhys ap Maredudd's revolt of 1287. Edward I stayed here for two nights in 1285. After the death of William de Braose II in 1321 there followed an extraordinarily complex series of events; it passed first to John de Mowbray who rebelled against Edward II and was executed; to Hugh Despenser, Lord of Glamorgan; to Elizabeth de Burgh, the ultimate de Braose heiress, and back to Alina de Mowbray (d.1331), her son John, and then to Thomas Beauchamp, Earl of Warwick. The Mowbrays returned in 1397. In the sixteenth century the Somerset Earls of Worcester gained the lordship of Glamorgan, and from them it eventually passed to the Dukes of Beaufort. In 1927 they sold it to Swansea council.

Oystermouth Castle.

• **Buildings** Today's ruins are the result of a long series of additions and rebuildings by many owners between 1215 and the fourteenth century. The fine gatehouse was built in the late thirteenth century; it has a peculiar shape, since the external flanking towers seem to have been completely dismantled, leaving two fluted concavities. The curtain walls with their accessible walkways must belong to the same period. The original keep has been much modified, and to the right or east was added the substantial fourteenth century chapel block, with four fine tracery windows and a delicate piscina. To the left or west of the keep is an intricacy of passages and smaller rooms. Despite the forbidding exterior of the castle and the usual claustrophobic feel of the main ward, the castle was clearly adapted for comfortable living.

ST DONAT'S

SS 935 681. Atlantic College.

• **Access** Although this unforgettable castle is hidden away at the end of several unclassified turnings off the B4265 between Llantwit Major and St Bride's Major, it is not hard to find. More difficult is to take the few chances available for a tour of the splendid buildings, namely on Sunday afternoons in July and August. Other opportunities may sometimes be available; e-mail enquiries@atlanticcollege.org or telephone 01446 799000. The castle and environs are home to Atlantic College, an international boarding school of high reputation, and to the St Donat's Arts Centre. Do not miss visiting the fine church in the *cwm* below the castle, including the undamaged medieval cross behind the building, a rarity indeed. On a fine day the wooded surrounds, cliffs and sea make this a special place.

St Donat's, resembling a fortified Oxbridge college.

• **History** The original twelfth-century castle was much altered *c*.1300 after the heiress Joan de Hawey married Peter de Stratelinges. It is claimed that his surname, anglicised as Stradling, was of Swiss derivation. His dynasty endured for four uninterrupted centuries, enabling the gradual development of the castle as a major country seat. Successive heads of the family were knighted and held numerous posts of responsibility. During the later sixteenth-century the family were staunch Catholics. The most notable of the family was Sir Edward Stradling (1529–1609), a gentleman-scholar of great distinction. His adopted son and heir John Stradling was also a scholar, which did not prevent him from fighting at the battle of Edgehill in 1642. The last Stradling, Sir Thomas, was killed in a duel in France in 1738; the estate was divided up and the fine library sold off.

Although the place fell into decline in the later eighteenth century it was never abandoned, and it was brought into good repair by Morgan Stuart Williams of Aberpergwm (d.1909). In 1925, it was bought by the notorious American newpaper proprietor William Randolph Hearst, whose career was the model for Orson Welles's great film *Citizen Kane*. Hearst employed Sir Charles Allom to redesign the castle's interior in the lavish style he favoured, using features ripped out of medieval buildings elsewhere, especially Bradenstoke Priory in Somerset, which lost its western cloister range with guest house and prior's lodging, and the whole tithe barn, all brought to St Donat's! In 1962 Atlantic College, founded by Kurt Hahn of Gordonstoun fame, became the first of a dozen United World Colleges and continues to enjoy great success.

• **Buildings** Although well-walled and strongly gated, the whole feeling of St Donat's is intimate rather than intimidating. Its plan is concentric; a low fortified gatehouse in the outer wall (both *c*.1300) leads to a simpler and earlier gateway, which with its Mansell tower is 12th century, as are the remaining inner curtain walls, all of local Liassic limestone. The inner court strongly resembles an attractive Oxbridge college; all is a delightful fifteen/sixteenth-century combination of limestone with Sutton and sandstone dressings. The interesting wall-busts in roundels were not part of the Hearst plunder but may have been here since the sixteenth century; the Great Hall on the south-east side of the court is earlier. Following round clockwise from the hall, Hearst's pillage predominates; the rooms include materials from several medieval English churches as well as a thirteenth-century seven-bay ceiling from Bradenstoke Hall.

SWANSEA

SS 657 931. Open access.

• **Access** Castle Street at the heart of the city is best reached either down High Street from the railway station, or from car parks in Kingsway. The site is more salubrious than it once was, and the fragments are impressive. Visiting is easier on a Sunday; it can be combined with visits either to the Swansea Museum, the National Maritime Museum and the Dylan Thomas Centre (all three close together), or with Oystermouth and the Gower castles.

• **History** The site lies above a low cliff below which the Tawe once flowed, and protected the main east-west route along the coast of south Wales. Swansea was the centre of the lordship of Gower, which included not only the peninsula of that name but also a similar-sized area northwards. Henry I granted the lordship to Henry de Beaumont in 1106; by 1116 it was being attacked by the Welsh, who eventually razed it in 1217, having failed in 1192. After it had suffered during Rhys ap

The last fragment of Swansea's might.

Maredudd's 1287 revolt a new castle was begun, of which the present remains formed a part. Although garrisoned against Glyndŵr's rebellion, it was not attacked and played no part in the Civil Wars. The site was always in demand; a mansion was built there in the fifteenth century; part became a poor-house and ventures in copper processing and glass manufacture occurred here. At one time there was a market, then a town hall; the militia were accommodated on site, part was used as a Roman Catholic chapel, and eventually it became the home of the *South Wales Evening Post*. It is now city property, cared for by Cadw.

• **Buildings**   Two parts of the castle remain, connected by a curtain wall. The splendid wall with its fine arcading still dominates the immediate neighbourhood despite the tower block behind it. This was the outer wall of a residential block, with a prominent garderobe tower at the west end. The small rectangular tower to the north has vaulted chambers below (no access), and was eventually used as a debtors' prison.

MERIONETHSHIRE

CASTELL Y BERE

SH 669 085. Open access.

• **Access**   The quiet but dramatically beautiful Dysynni valley is in itself an attraction, and to Welsh people the tiny village of Llanfihangel-y-Pennant, just beyond the castle rock, has a special appeal as the home of Mary Jones, youthful inspirer of the creation of the Bible Society. On entering the valley from the A493 via either Tywyn or Llanegryn, the valley is dominated by Craigyderyn (Bird Rock), for long the only inland nesting place in Britain for cormorants. Further on another rocky mass rises from the valley bottom, much of it covered in trees which in summer hide the castle ruins. The castle itself is so wrecked that it is barely visible from a distance unless one were to climb the steep hills on either side. A small rough car park leads to a footpath athwart the rock, which eventually winds round to

Castell y Bere, looking north-eastwards.
Photograph: Paul Davis.

a flight of wooden steps between substantial defences which still look formidable.

• **History** Deep in the heartland of Gwynedd, this castle was commissioned by Llywelyn the Great in 1221 after seizing Meirionnydd (the land between Mawddach and Dyfi) from his son Gruffudd. Following the death of Llywelyn ap Gruffudd in December 1282 his brother Dafydd attempted to continue the struggle, first here, then at Dolbadarn. In May 1283 Castell y Bere's Welsh governor put up no resistance to Edward's generals, selling his charge for the generous sum of £80. Edward ordered money spent on improvements, but in the fierce revolt of Madog ap Llywelyn in 1294–5 the castle was burnt and abandoned. Outside the west end the pocked and hummocky ground indicates a degree of settlement, but whether this can be attributed to pre- or post-1283 cannot be determined, though the earlier date is likely.

Buildings The vistor enters by the outer gate past the
barbican to the inner gate, with a round tower on the left and
what is probably a cistern rather than a well immediately in
front. On the right are steps up to an oblong keep; this leads
through a small courtyard to the south tower, which could have
served as a separate keep if the main castle were breached.
The walls joining the south tower to the keep were probably
built during the brief Edwardian occupation. The masonry is
of local volcanic rock. Returning to the courtyard, one can
see the foundations of buildings against the curtain walls on
either side. Finally the north or chapel tower is reached. The
castle gives splendid views north-eastwards towards Cadair
Idris and south-westwards down the lovely Dysynni valley.

HARLECH

SH 581 312. Cadw. Fee.

• **Access** One of the four World Heritage Edwardian castles in
Wales, Harlech stands on a mighty rock looking seaward, and
behind it straggles the original little town, which once claimed
medieval borough status. The sea once reached the great crag,
but centuries of sand now separate them, giving space for the
town to expand. It can be reached by the Cambrian Coast rail
line (short, very steep walk from the station) or by bus and by
car off the A496. There is a small car park at the castle with
a visitor centre, and a larger car park with a 5–8 minute walk
is signed not far away. There are permanent displays on show
inside the huge gate-towers and at certain summer weekends
there are plays and re-enactments.

• **History** There is no sign of fortification pre-1283, but the
rock (*hardd-lech* = lovely stone) was celebrated in Welsh

Harlech Castle.

legend as a court of the giant ruler of Britain, Bendigeidfran. Here Matholwch, king of Ireland, came to seek the hand in marriage of Branwen, the king's sister, in the finest and saddest of the Four Branches of the Mabinogion. Of all Edward's castles designed to cow the Welsh into submission, this was the one that saw most warfare in the following centuries. Edward's troops reached Harlech in 1283 and building work was put in hand almost immediately. A remarkable feature of the castle was the inclusion within the main south wall of the timber hall of the Welsh *llys* or court at Ystumgwern to the south of Harlech, perhaps symbolising the end of Welsh rule and the triumph of English. Within six years the work was largely complete, at a cost of more than £8,000, and it successfully withstood its first siege during the fierce revolt of Madog ap Llywelyn in 1294, thanks to supplies shipped from

Ireland. One consequence of the siege was the creation of a wall around the foot of the great rock itself with a water-gate at its base, necessary at that time when the sea still lapped around the site.

Owain Glyndŵr's first attempt to capture Harlech in 1401 failed, but renewed attack succeeded in 1404 and Harlech became a major centre of Glyndŵr's Welsh rule. His coat of arms, the four lions rampant originally adopted by the princes of Gwynedd, appears on a bronze mount discovered in the castle in 1923. The English eventually starved the Welsh defenders out in 1409, though Owain escaped at the cost of abandoning his wife and children. Fifty years later Harlech was a major centre of Lancastrian power in the Wars of the Roses, withstanding siege for seven years, until the garrison finally surrendered in 1468. Nearly two centuries later it became the last castle in Wales held for Charles I in the Civil Wars, until it too succumbed in 1647. Parliamentarian instructions to slight the castle were ineffective, and the onslaught of stone-robbers which might have been expected hardly happened.

• **Buildings**   The massive rock-cut ditch was dug early in the building process, providing protection for the English builders but making access for building supplies more awkward. The plan is trapezoidal and concentric; a narrow outer ward separates the outer and inner curtain walls. The whole is dominated by the giant gate-tower which replaced the keep of earlier generations of castle planning, and is to the design of Master James of St George, who eventually became constable of the castle. The entrance was defended by the ditch, by a double drawbridge and then three doors and three portcullises in the gateway itself. The accommodation, for its time, was splendid, with fireplaces in the living apartments, separate bedrooms and many latrines. All the masonry is local sandstone; the dressing stones are from nearby Egryn.

Inside the ward were buildings on three sides; the Ystumgwern hall to the south, the great hall and kitchens to the west and a chapel in the north-west corner. Stairs still give access to the magnificent wall-walk. The north-east tower has a dungeon. The western towers were built rather later than the rest of the castle to the design of Master William of Drogheda.

TOMEN-Y-MUR

SH 703 387. On private land, but a public footpath gives access.

• **Access** A narrow driveable lane climbs eastward from the A470 just south of its junction with the A701 to Ffestiniog for a kilometre and more before reaching an area where a few cars can park. The motte can be reached on a footpath.

• **History and Site** One of the most exposed and bleak sites

Tomen-y-mur's motte clearly visible within the Roman fort. Crown copyright RCAHMW.

anywhere in Wales, Tomen-y-Mur resonates in Welsh culture and history. The castle itself is a simple motte and bailey, but its situation squarely within a Roman fort, and its place in the legend of Lleu Llaw Gyffes, suffering hero of the Fourth Branch of the Mabinogion, make the site special. Here in his own court Lleu was betrayed, Samson-like, by his wife Blodeuwedd, the woman made from flowers. The Roman remains are extensive; outside the ramparts of the fort itself one can see the footings of the bathhouse and a bridge, the remains of the *mansio* (inn), the parade ground and amphitheatre, as well as water leats. The late eleventh-century motte is comparatively commonplace, but early mottes are rare in north-west Wales; it marks the vain attempt of William II in 1095 to quell the Welsh insurgency of the period. Nothing else is known of its history.

MONMOUTHSHIRE

ABERGAVENNY

SO 299 139. County Council. Open access.

• **Access** Walk from the town's main, busy car park towards town centre, turn left at Lower Castle Street, following signs for the castle. Do not miss the town's splendid priory church, a glory of architecture and medieval sculpture.

• **History** Castle and borough were founded *c*.1090 by Hamelin de Ballon at a major crossing of routes from Newport, Monmouth and Brecon. It was rebuilt in stone *c*.1175. Scene of William de Braose's slaughter through the treachery of a number of leading Welshmen of Gwent, the Welsh avenged the massacre by destroying most of the castle in 1182. It was

Geoffrey of Monmouth's 'Night of the Long Knives' may have inspired William de Braose's treachery at Abergavenny.

stormed in 1215 and destroyed in 1233 by Llywelyn the Great, rebuilt by William Cantilupe. Charles I ordered its destruction in 1645.

• **Buildings** Visitors enter through the remains of the gatehouse, passing into the outer ward. The foundations of the hall can be seen on the left against the late thirteenth-century wall. The next gateway leads into the inner ward, and on the left are the most substantial fragments, those of the solar tower. The motte, where once the keep stood, is now crowned by an early nineteenth-century hunting lodge which contains the pleasant local museum, well worth a visit.

CALDICOT

ST 487 885. County Council. Fee.

• **Access** This pleasant castle is on the east side of Caldicot. Leave the M4 at junction 23a and follow the B4245 to Caldicot.

There are road signs to the castle, but the actual entrance, near the parish church, is rather obscure. Drive through the country park to the castle. Caldicot castle has charm rather than menace, not having been hygienized and deodorized like its magnificent neighbour Chepstow. The walls still sprout flowers and ivy; its moat is empty but muddy. Photographers cannot easily photograph its fine façade for the splendid cedar trees of the pleasant country park in which the castle now stands. Since it is council-owned and managed it lacks the wide publicity that Cadw can give to its many buildings. Caldicot may not rank among the greatest Welsh castles, but few are better suited to family visits; it has its own tea-room, there are outdoor draughts and chess to play, and child-friendly dressing-up rooms in the Woodstock tower. Parking is free; there is a good footpath round the outside of the complex, a welcome at the door, and an audio-guided tour is available.

Caldicot's Victorian living quarters.

• **History**   The original motte on which the keep now stands was probably established by William fitz Osbern, Earl of Hereford, when he swept across the Gwentian plain in 1067. It soon passed, obscurely, to Walter fitz Roger, who held the grand title of Constable of England. His son Milo became earl of Hereford but had no son, so his daughter Margaret took her father's titles, and Caldicot, to her husband Humphrey Bohun in 1158. Later the family gained the earldoms of Essex and Northampton. Successive Bohuns played major parts in the national history of England for the next two centuries until their possessions passed by the marriage of Alianore Bohun to Thomas of Woodstock, , Duke of Gloucester, youngest son of Edward III, in 1376. Thomas, after building extensively at Caldicot, was assassinated on the orders of his nephew Richard II. Alianore's sister Mary married Henry Bolingbroke, who in 1399 became Henry IV, and Mary's son, Henry V, was born at Monmouth. Ownership passed to the Herberts and then the Somersets of Raglan. The castle, never attacked or besieged, fell into ruin until it was bought by Joseph Richard Cobb in 1885, who began its restoration. The Cobb family sold it to Chepstow Rural District Council in 1963.

• **Buildings**   The splendid fourteenth century great gatehouse was remodelled by JR Cobb to be his home; medieval-style banquets are now held in the great hall upstairs. The protruding towers flanking the gate, the drawbridge and murder holes gave the defenders considerable control over would-be attackers. Turning left from the tower to walk the circuit, the walls (mid-thirteenth century) are still complete, though ruinous. The south-west tower, partly rebuilt (early twentieth century) is contemporary with the walls, as is the next feature, the Bohun gate, whose powerful defences are still clear to see. The towers would have given fine views over the surrounding countryside, which would have been at least partially landscaped, with deer park, orchard and fishponds.

Then comes the keep, the oldest stonework in the castle (possibly early thirteenth century), around whose walls earth has been piled up so that the cellar is actually at ground level. It is also suggested that this earthwork was the original motte, but that seems unlikely, though proof is lacking either way. Caldicot's masonry is of calcareous sandstone, with Sudbrook dressings. Surviving documents show that the Woodstock tower was built in 1385–86 by Thomas of Woodstock. Ignoring the modern gateway on the east, the last (south-east) tower is fourteenth century. Between it and the Great Gatehouse was the original hall and service complex. The massive cannon on the lawn belonged to HMS *Foudroyant*, a wooden battleship of the Napoleonic wars bought by JR Cobb; it was wrecked off Blackpool in 1897.

CHEPSTOW

ST 533 941. Cadw. Fee.

• **Access**   The A48 runs through the middle of the attractive town of Chepstow, crossing the Wye, which is the Anglo–Welsh boundary. The splendid castle lies on a long ridge just off Bridge Street, with a convenient paying car park, tourist information centre, guidebook available and the excellent Chepstow museum opposite.

• **History**   This fine dramatic castle on its great cliff above the river was the first to be commenced in Wales. William fitz Osbern, Earl of Hereford (d.1071), crossed the Wye in 1067 with royal encouragement and began building, though what he built is still disputed. Most sources attribute the stone hall-keep to him, and he certainly founded the priory whose church now serves the town and is well worth a visit. Fitz Osbern's son, Roger, lost his earldom in 1075 following a conspiracy against

Chepstow's hall-keep.

the king, who retained the castle for the Crown. In 1115 it was granted along with its lordship of Striguil to Walter fitz Richard of Clare (d.1138), founder of Tintern Abbey. From Walter it passed to his nephew Gilbert de Clare, and by the marriage of his daughter to William Marshall (d.1219), who extended the building considerably.

Chepstow passed one by one through the hands of Marshall's five childless sons until the death of the last, Anselm, in 1245, and then to Roger Bigood (d.1306), son of one of Marshall's daughters, Earl of Norfolk and marshal of England. He continued the extension of the castle to its present remarkable extent, bankrupting himself in the process, he gave generously to Tintern Abbey. Intriguingly, the castle was never attacked during the whole medieval period, not even during Glyndŵr's revolt, which saw fierce fighting at Monmouth. Only at the time of the Civil Wars was the castle twice defended by its owners, the royalist Somersets of Raglan, in 1645 and again in 1648. After its second capture by Cromwell's forces it became a prison, holding among others the divine and author Jeremy Taylor and the regicide Henry Martyn.

The irony of this magnificent castle never having had to withstand medieval attack could be attributed to its deterrent effect; it has been seen as strategically essential to the Norman conquest of south Wales. But this corner of Wales was never threatened by the Welsh even at the heights of their many insurgencies, and it can equally be looked on as an assertion of status and power by successive Marcher lords who held other great castles, especially Pembroke, as well as estates in England.

• **Buildings** Chepstow's first great rectangular tower, whether commenced in 1067 or later, is an intriguing building. The hall was at first floor level, resembling a huge reception area as much as it does the keep of a military castle. Roman brick was used as an occasional alternative to the limestone masonry, and the archwayed entrance looks more prestigious than defensive. The hall would have impressed visitors with its painted stucco and blind arcading. The first ward was that now known as the Middle Ward. The Marshalls improved the hall and living quarters, while also fortifying the lower ward and building a gatehouse, creating a gallery between the great hall and cliff edge. Round towers, perhaps the first in Wales, appeared in the bailey walls and rebuilt gatehouse. The castle was extended westwards beyond the great hall to include an upper bailey and magnificent barbican at the furthest end. The dressing stones are from Sudbrook.

Roger Bigood's contribution was to strengthen the barbican in the west, to complete the second storey of the great hall begun by the Marshalls with a new range of domestic buildings and building a large D-shaped tower in the lower ward. The tower was intended as Bigood's domestic accommodation, and it was there that the regicide Henry Martyn was held for twenty years, giving his name to the tower. Bigood also built Chepstow's borough walls of which part survives, including the great gate. Further additions and sophistications were added by the Somersets in the sixteenth century, though it was never their main residence.

NEWPORT

ST 312 885. Cadw. Open access.

• **Access**   Best seen from the train east of the station, or visited on a Sunday when parking is just possible nearby.

• **History**   This sad wreck was a major castle, centre of the lordship of Newport, built in the fourteenth century, much reshaped in the fifteenth. The Monmouthshire canal (vanished) was dug through the site in the eighteenth century. During the nineteenth century it was used as a brewery, tannery and nail factory.

• **Buildings**   What remains is the Usk river frontage, always the castle's major feature. Flanked by corner towers once containing apartments, the main feature is the water gate. Unfortunately its fine vaulted presence chamber has a repellent urban reek, this in spite of Cadw's good landscaping of the approach. The water gate allowed boats to sail right into the entrance to unload men and provisions, a useful reminder of Newport's long maritime history.

Newport's river frontage, the watergate centre.

RAGLAN

SO 414 083. Cadw. Fee.

• **Access** Thanks to its position at the junction of the A40 with the A449 routeway, but not in a built-up area, Raglan is one of the most accessible of southern Welsh castles, and one of the finest. Its massive complexity and its rural situation, as well as its historic rôle in the Civil Wars, make it especially attractive to visitors; it should soon have the visitors' centre it deserves. The splendid seventeenth-century farmhouse close by has a franchised tearoom. Whereas the history and architecture of many castles can be problematical for scholars and speculative for visitors, Raglan is so well-documented, so interesting and complex that it is wise to buy the official guide, not least for the anecdotes it contains of the 1646 siege.

Raglan: the last great medieval Welsh castle.

• **History**   Raglan in its heyday was as much a palace as a
castle. It began simply enough as an early motte and bailey,
held by Walter Bloet, one of the knight-followers of Richard
de Clare (Strongbow, d.1176). About 1390 the Bloet heiress's
second husband, William ap Thomas, gained possession,
and it was he or his son who began the moated Great Tower
('the Yellow Tower of Gwent'). His son, Sir William Herbert,
continued his father's building work while becoming one of the
great men of the kingdom, having virtually assured the Yorkist
Edward IV's succession in 1461 after the battle of Mortimer's
Cross. Made Earl of Pembroke in 1468, he was executed after
the Lancastrian victory at the battle of Edgecote the following
year.

In 1492 the Earl's granddaughter Elizabeth took Raglan

and its broad estates to her husband Charles Somerset, Earl of Worcester and ancestor of the dukes of Beaufort. Raglan castle was much improved by the third Earl, who with his son created splendid gardens around the castle, of which there is now no trace. During the Civil Wars the fifth earl of Worcester, a man of vast wealth and a Roman Catholic, helped finance Charles I's military campaigns against Parliament until forced to surrender the castle after a six-week siege in 1646; he died later in captivity. Thereafter, following the abandonment by the parliamentarian authorities of their efforts to destroy the castle, the Somerset family (Dukes of Beaufort after 1756, with their home at Badminton but retaining large estates in Wales) cleared and repaired the ruins before eventually handing it over to the Ministry of Works in 1938.

• **Buildings** Pass through the gatehouse (1460s), with its gunloops, murder holes and portcullises to the splendid pitched court, surrounded by the remains of the sixteenth-century service buildings. 'Pitched' refers to the slopes from the raised centre, allowing ready drainage. The office wing (sixteenth century) reaches from the fifteenth-century Closet Tower on the right down to the kitchen tower (fifteenth century); the original wing joining the two was replaced by the third earl of Worcester. This wing was badly damaged by parliamentarian bombardment in the 1646 siege. From the kitchen tower, move leftwards to the Pantry, Buttery and Hall (mid-sixteenth century). A first-floor dining-room was used by the family, nobility and knights; the Hall was for household officials and senior servants. It was once splendidly roofed with Irish oak.

A passage leads to the fountain court, now lacking its fountain and ornamental parterres. It is surrounded on three sides by the fifteenth century-apartment buildings created by Sir William Herbert, which would in their time have been the acme of luxury. Each chamber had a fireplace and access to latrines, whose waste must have made the moat noisome in summer. On the fourth side is the largely destroyed chapel which would have been the spiritual centre of the family's life; the Somersets were loyal Catholics throughout the Tudor and early Stuart period. Above the chapel and buttery ran the long gallery, whose splendour is still faintly indicated by two sculpted human figures, one male, one female. They are decorative caryatids, not portraits.

The focal point of the apartment buildings is the grand staircase, now ruinous. To the left is the south gateway (early fifteenth century), briefly a main entrance before its replacement by the gatehouse; it led to the castle's bowling green. The most important of the apartments, called the State Apartments, lay behind the hall where visitors now cross to the great tower. This was where the Earls (later Marquesses) of Worcester conducted their domestic lives and political affairs; the area is now ruinous.

The Great Tower itself (c.1435–45) is the castle's most impressive single building. With its moat and drawbridge it was originally a freestanding castle; Sir William Herbert felt sufficiently secure within the extensions to replace the original drawbridge with stone (the present bridge is modern). Far from allowing it to fall into ruin, it was well-maintained while he and his successors built the rest of the present complex. The tower's rooms may well have been a retreat for family members from the hurly-burly of castle life. The collapse of part of the tower was brought about deliberately after its capture by Sir Thomas Fairfax, but it was so troublesome that the planned destruction of the whole complex was abandoned. The view from the top is well worth the trouble of climbing the stairs; the visitor should try to imagine the present lawns as splendid Renaissance gardens.

THE THREE CASTLES OF GWENT

Grosmont

Skenfrith

White Castle *SO 379 168.*

All three open daily; no fee.

• **Access**   These three fine castles are treated in a single Cadw guide, and are so closely related by geography and history as to deserve joint treatment; they make a pleasant triangular excursion by car in an afternoon, or a whole day on the Three Castles walk. Do not attempt the tour without a reasonable map. Don't miss the splendid church at Skenfrith, with its rare medieval embroidered cope. If starting by car from Abergavenny, follow the B4521 until you see signs for White Castle on the right. This is the most remote of the three, the only one without a village. If starting from Monmouth, follow the B4233 to Rockfield and the B4347 onward to a crossroads with the B4521; turn right for Skenfrith. Grosmont is further north on the B4347, at the northern apex of the triangle.

• **History**   Once William fitz Osbern (d.1071) had begun the castles at Monmouth and Chepstow, the next Norman move was into the rolling land between the rivers Monnow and Usk. William's early death and his son's revolt against the Crown in 1075 meant that the area passed into the king's hands. After a period when it was divided between royal followers, the area including Grosmont, Skenfrith and White Castle (sometimes called Llantilio in the records) was brought together in a single lordship by King Stephen (d.1154). The Three Castles lordship remained a unit for many centuries. There is no reference to the castles themselves until 1162, but since this involved garrison expenses and repairs, and since earthworks of early Norman pattern were created at all three sites, it is clear that there were motte and bailey castles here well before 1100. The foundations of a small square keep survive at White Castle, probably the earliest stonework in any of the three. The Welsh threat in the 1180s brought more strengthening and rebuilding in stone.

In 1201 King John granted the Three Castles to Hubert de Burgh (d.1243), who rose to be one of the greatest of Anglo-Norman barons. He began the rebuilding of Grosmont and Skenfrith, modernising their accommodation, using his experience of campaigning in France. A man of his position and power had many enemies, and more than once he lost control of his Welsh castles and lands (including Montgomery, Cardigan and Carmarthen); his building work was probably complete by 1232, when Hubert was turned out of office and castles. This brought Richard Marshall of Chepstow and Usk to his aid; Henry III marched against him from Gloucester and camped his army outside Grosmont castle. Richard's men fell on him in the darkness, and king and army fled back to Gloucester.

Hubert's castles were held for the king by Walerund the German, who added accommodation buildings at White Castle and a chapel at Skenfrith. After his and Hubert's deaths the Three Castles passed in 1254 to the Lord Edward, the future King Edward I, and in 1267 from him to his brother Edmund of Lancaster. The rise of Llywelyn ap Gruffudd to rule most of Wales threatened English control of Gwent, and White Castle was remodelled and strengthened. The Welsh threat died with Llywelyn in 1282, only to be reborn with Owain Glyndŵr's revolt; Welsh rebels were defeated in 1404 at Campston Hill near Grosmont, and Owain's son besieged Grosmont castle in 1405, without success. That was the end of the military history of the Three Castles; they played no part in the Civil Wars. The Duchy of Lancaster sold the whole lordship in 1825 to the Duke of Beaufort; in 1902 the three castles were sold separately.

Grosmont   *SO 405 244. Open daily; no fee.* What is now a pleasant village was once a borough, with mayor and corporation, and a fine church. As so often, the castle is badly signposted; it lies a hundred yards to the east of the village street, accessed by footpath. The castle site once covered a larger area whose outer boundary is not easily traced. The modern footbridge crosses the fine ditch through the ruined gatehouse into the inner ward on the original motte, with the early thirteenth-century hall block on the right and the later curtain wall and towers in front and on the left. Like Skenfrith, the whole building is of local red sandstone, which could be used for windows and doorways as well as walls. The hall itself was at the first storey level, with timber flooring, and beyond it a solar or private withdrawing room for the lord and his family.

*Grosmont,
from the south.*

The towers on the west side of the castle, originally by Hubert de Burgh, were extensively remodelled in the fourteenth century under the Lancaster administration. A tall octagonal chimney of the same period dominates the north block, which is a complete remodelling of an original tower built by de Burgh, only the foundations of which survive. The inner ward must have been a claustrophobic place; not only is it small and still surrounded by high walls, but much of the space would have been filled with timber buildings. Care is needed on the flights of rugged steps leading up to a section of wall-walk.

Skenfrith *ST 457 203. Open daily; no fee.* Skenfrith is a considerable contrast to Grosmont. For a start, it is well signposted, though since its massive bulk lies next to the main road it would be hard to miss. It is sited on level ground beside the river Monnow, which would have supplied the castle's moat, now filled in, so that the walls now look more approachable than they once were. They would have been especially menacing to enemies, since on the outer walls and the corner towers were fighting galleries made of timber, whose support-holes still survive. The original motte-and-bailey was entirely levelled to provide a building platform for Hubert de Burgh's early thirteenth-century castle. The gateway in the NW wall is now only a gap. There is a small entrance low in the east wall, apparently a water-gate.

The four corner towers survive; since they had no fireplaces or latrines their purpose was purely defensive. The windowless and doorless ground level spaces in the towers may have been used for storage, though they were (and are) subject to flooding. The NE tower still has one arrowloop window for defence; stones from the others have been robbed. At the centre of the inner ward is a round keep with strong battered (outward sloping) walls with some of the original white plaster

Skenfrith from the air. Crown copyright RCAHMW.

still in place. The present entrance replaces the original first floor doorway, which was accessed by a timber stairway. A bulge on the SW side of the tower contains a spiral stair to reach the second and third storeys from the first. The upper chamber had a large fireplace and its own latrine, probably the lord's accommodation. Around the top of the keep would have been another timber fighting gallery, whose height would enable archers to fire over the curtain walls at any besiegers.

Archaeology has revealed a good deal of detail from the buildings which once partly filled the inner ward. On the right of the gateway was a hall range of three chambers at first-floor level. Masons' marks can be seen on the doorway at the foot of the sloping path, while in the window on the descent can be seen the original medieval ironwork. Elsewhere in the ward can be seen the foundations of an oven, and the site of the kitchen, though nothing of this survives above ground.

White Castle *SO 379 168. Open daily; no fee.* This is the largest of the three castles. Its splendid site, looking far to the south, and its fine walls and towers, are a little odd: there is no civilian settlement close by, nor apparently has there ever been. The nearest village, Llantilio Crossenny, is a mile away. Some Welsh-built stone castles appear isolated in their landscapes, but Norman stone castles are rarely if ever so alone. White Castle may have been more important as a military centre than as comfortable accommodation for the lords of the Three Castles.

The ground plan is complex. When visitors reach the present outer gatehouse, they are actually already passing from one half of the outer ward into the other, walled half. Outside these walls is a dry moat. The now empty space within these walls was once full of timber buildings for stores and accommodation. At the centre of the plan, entirely surrounded by a fine moat revetted in stone, is the main castle, reached across a bridge and through a splendid twin-towered gatehouse. It is possible to climb the NW tower and enjoy views in all directions.

The inner ward was originally reached, not from the north

*White Castle
from the north.*

as at present, but from the south through what is now a gap in the curtain wall, but was an archwayed entrance. Next to the gap are the massive foundations of a small Norman keep, which like the curtain walls is twelfth century in origin, and was demolished a century later, when towers were added to the walls. Within the walls, starting anti-clockwise from the main gatehouse, were the kitchen and brewhouse, while opposite them were the hall, a well and a solar. From the gap in the walls one can see the fine hornwork, a large crescent-shaped bank which now can only be accessed by crossing a narrow and dangerous stone dam athwart the moat – not recommended! The hornwork is itself surrounded by the moat on all sides, and once had timber palisades and towers, as well as bridges enabling the twin moats to be crossed.

USK

SO 377 010. Private ownership. Open access.

• **Access** Usk castle today is a hidden place. Unmarked on road atlases, almost entirely unpublicised, ignored even by many of those who turn off the A48 dual carriageway to enjoy this charming little town, Usk castle on a warm spring day is a revelation. Ignore all the leaflets which insist that the castle can only be seen by appointment, and go; it is always open, as the excellent website, www.uskcastle.com, will tell you. The poorly-signed entrance is on the right-hand (north) side of the slip road from the A48 just before entering the town, and up the short drive there is a car park. At the castle entrance is an honesty box and a useful guide leaflet.

• **History**   The castle's early history is frustratingly vague. It is first mentioned in the mid-1130s, when Morgan ab Owain of Caerleon seized it from the powerful de Clare family after the death of the head of the family. Welsh possession was

Usk Castle. Crown copyright RCAHMW.

disputed by Richard de Clare ('Strongbow', d.1176) who held it for a period or periods. Hywel ab Iorwerth of Caerleon appears to have resumed Welsh control until 1183, when he was betrayed and killed. In 1189 William Marshall assumed ownership in the right of his wife Isabel, the de Clare heiress. The date of the stone keep is conjectural; it could be the work of Richard de Clare, it might even be the work of the Welsh lords of Caerleon; alternatively it may have been Marshall's first contribution to the stonework. Later, although occupied with great affairs of state, Marshall found time to order the building of the walls and towers surrounding the inner ward, probably between 1212 and his death in 1219, when Llywelyn the Great was a threat to the southern Marcher lords.

William Marshall had no grandsons, so Usk reverted to a branch of the de Clares, Earls of Gloucester and Lords of Glamorgan. The last of them, Gilbert, died at Bannockburn in 1314 but not before he and/or his father, Gilbert the Red, had added considerably to the defences and begun the major domestic block and chapel of the early fourteenth century, completed by the younger Gilbert's widow Matilda by her death in 1320. The eventual de Clare heiress was Gilbert's sister Elizabeth (de Burgh by her first marriage), who lived here on and off until her death in 1360, surviving an attempt by Edward II's doomed favourites the de Spensers to deprive her of castle and lordship. Elizabeth herself, a great lady of her day, was responsible for extensive repairs and alterations *c.*1350. After her death Usk passed to Edmund Mortimer (d.1381), who added the gatehouse, outer ward and dovecote tower.

Usk town was burnt in 1402 by Glyndŵr's followers; a horrible revenge was exacted when his men were defeated at nearby Pwll Melyn in 1405 and three hundred Welsh prisoners were slaughtered. The castle may have survived the Welsh attack, but control of the lordship of Usk passed from the Mortimers to Richard, Duke of York, and was granted to William ap Thomas of Raglan. After the 1469 execution of William's grandson William Herbert, Earl of Pembroke, it came into royal hands for a century before passing back to the Herberts.

• **Buildings** At its most extensive the castle had three main divisions, the outer or southern ward, the inner ward and the northern ward. The visitor enters past the present owner's house (incorporating the gatehouse) to reach the trapezoidal twelfth-century keep, with its later modifications. Around the inner ward, which is now a delightful garden with lawnmowing geese, the main features are the massive garrison tower facing the entrance, and the north range. The former was the central element of William Marshal's extensions, comparable in form to the huge towers at Bronllys and Tretower. It is possible to climb to the wall-walk. The masonry is of local limestone.

To the north is Gilbert de Clare's pre-1289 tower, where his treasure was kept, as well as the chapel, hall and chamber block of the fourteenth century. The roofless chapel contains the grave of the present owner's parents and is occasionally used for services. There are fine views southwards from the inner ward, and immediately below the curtain wall is a fine private garden in the outer ward and a splendid barn building. The northern ward awaits archaeological examination.

MONTGOMERYSHIRE

DOLFORWYN

SO 152 950. Open access.

• **Access** This magnificent site well repays the trouble it takes to reach. From the A483 turn north-west at SO 162 953 on an unclassified road past the entrance to the Dolforwyn Hall hotel, turn left and keep on to the tiny signed car park on the left. The path on the right leads steeply up and then athwart the slope to emerge among the hummocks of the short-lived medieval Welsh borough. Thirty years ago there was little to be seen here, but excavations in the 1980s unearthed a remarkable Welsh-built castle which had become buried in its own collapsed rubble. There is a good Cadw guidebook for Dolforwyn and Montgomery; the two castles make an excellent joint excursion, and the guidebook can be bought in Montgomery.

• **History**   Llywelyn ap Gruffudd's growing power in the 1250s and 1260s brought him to the territory of Cedewain, disputed between the local prince Gruffudd ap Gwenwynwyn and Roger Mortimer, greatest of the contemporary Marcher lords. Both were Llywelyn's kinsmen. Llywelyn, recognised in 1267 by Henry III as Prince of Wales, began building a castle on the ridge above Dolforwyn ('Our Lady's Meadow') in 1273, with a new borough attached. The site enjoys splendid views over the Severn valley, and was immediately seen as a threat to the royal castle at Montgomery. Unusually in the case of a princely castle, we know the name of Llywelyn's castellan, Bleddyn ap Llywelyn, and that £173 6s. 8d. was spent on the work from April 1273 to April 1274. It was at Dolforwyn in 1274 that Llywelyn learnt of a plot against his life by his mercurial brother Dafydd and Gruffudd ap Gwenwynwyn, both resentful of Llywelyn's power. The two fled to the protection of Edward I, newly returned from crusade, so Llywelyn seized Gruffudd's lands.

Years earlier, the young Edward had suffered military humiliation at the hands of Llywelyn, ally of Edward's enemy Simon de Montfort. Now king, he sought to insist on the homage which Llywelyn owed him by the treaty of 1267, and held Llywelyn's wife-to-be, Eleanor de Montfort, captive at Windsor. His councillors had already rebuked the prince for building Dolforwyn. Llywelyn was enraged by Edward's behaviour and refused to do homage. Edward's campaign against Gwynedd began in 1277 with the siege of Dolforwyn and the burning of the little borough, led by Roger Mortimer and using large siege catapults which inflicted considerable damage with stone balls, several of which are to be seen on the site. The garrison surrendered and Edward granted Dolforwyn to Mortimer, who replaced the destroyed 'old town' with a borough at Newtown (hence the name), but maintained the castle.

When in 1322 Dolforwyn was confiscated from Mortimer ownership for a period, an inventory was made describing

The recovered interior of Llywelyn's Dolforwyn.

the buildings and contents in some detail, confirmed and extended by modern excavation. There was a lady's chamber in the round tower with a bathing tub; the hall was paved and plastered; there were stained glass windows. Finds included amber beads, hat badges, tuning pegs for a stringed instrument and an ivory book cover with the figure of a saint. Alterations were made by the Mortimer owners from time to time, but by 1381 the castle was in poor condition and played no known part in the Glyndŵr rebellion or later history.

• **Buildings** Once the summit of the ridge had been levelled, the masons commenced building a round tower at the northeast end and an oblong keep separately to the south-west; this is the largest tower known to have been built by any Welsh prince. The material is local Silurian sandstone, with dressing stone from Shropshire. Curtain walls linked the two to give a modified rhomboid plan. The large defensive ditches provided plenty of stone for the walls; it would be interesting to know how Llywelyn acquired sandstone for the dressings, fragments of which survive. Although the active life of the castle was barely a century, the Mortimer additions and the ravages of time make the site complicated for the visitor; fortunately there are useful display panels. While the ditches, curtain walls and towers were Welsh-built, many of the internal features were added after 1277.

The approach to the castle is from the south-west across the site of the borough. Visitors will enjoy walking right round the castle on the convenient shelf before entering where the gatehouse once stood, with the keep on the right. The courtyard was divided by a ditch giving access to the south entrance (now partly walled); it was originally crossed by a stone bridge.

MONTGOMERY

SO 221 968. Cadw. Open access.

• **Access** If you turn into the delightful little town square you may find room to park and then follow the signs up the hill. However a minor road will take you up to the small car park from which a footpath (no dogs) leads to the splendid site, with magnificent views across the Severn valley. There is a joint Cadw guidebook (with Dolforwyn) which can be bought in the town. If you are lucky the excellent little museum at the sign of the Old Bell will be open – don't miss it.

• **History**   On a low rise between Montgomery town and the river Severn, hidden by trees, is the mound of Hen Domen, whose modern excavation has shown how much archaeologists

Henry III's royal castle at Montgomery.

and historians can learn from an earth-castle site; there is a good exhibit in the museum. Hen Domen was built to guard the ford of Rhyd Chwima, a strategic site in the dealings of Welsh and English. It was reconstructed several times; the original foundation was by Roger of Montgomery from St Germain de Montgommeri in Normandy, giving Wales one of its few French place-names. Roger was earl of Shrewsbury, and this was his forward base for deep penetration into Wales, all the way to Cardigan.

During the twelfth century the Welsh of Powys managed to regain much of their territory, and by 1216 much of the district of Montgomery was under the control of Llywelyn ap Iorwerth. In 1223 royal forces succeeded in pushing the Welsh back across the Severn, and a new castle was begun on the much more defensible present site by order of the sixteen-year-old King Henry III, advised by the formidable Hubert de Burgh. A town was founded below the castle, which was twice burnt by Llywelyn ap Iorwerth, though the castle survived, and was given a royal charter in 1227.

The town was destroyed a third time by Llywelyn ap Gruffudd in 1257 as part of the dramatic expansion of his principality, though he did not hold on to the district. In 1267 he came to Rhyd Chwima to meet Henry III, who had agreed to recognise Llywelyn as Prince of Wales. Llywelyn would receive the homage of the lesser Welsh princes, and do homage to the king on their behalf. In 1273 he began his own castle of Dolforwyn, west of the Severn but only four miles from Montgomery, to strengthen his hold on southern Powys. This, together with Llywelyn's persistent refusal to do homage to the new king Edward I, brought the outbreak of war in 1277. Montgomery was a key base in Edward's devastating strategy which brought about Llywelyn's surrender. It was the main meeting centre for Edward's lawyers to examine the state of law in Wales.

Montgomery played a lesser rôle in the war of 1282–83 which finally destroyed Llywelyn, but it was again a key base in the campaign against the great revolt of Madog ap Llywelyn in 1294–95. The king granted the castle to the Mortimer family, who held it until 1425, with intervals of royal possession. It was garrisoned against the Glyndŵr revolt in 1402, but is not known to have been attacked. In the early sixteenth century the castle came into the hands of the Somerset-Herbert family. The Civil Wars brought swift parliamentarian capture in 1644, a royalist siege and a fierce battle below the castle between the parliamentarians and the royalist relief force, many of whom were massacred in the defeat that followed. This was not the end; in June 1645 the parliamentarian governor changed sides, only to renege after the king's defeat at Naseby. The castle, and the fine house built in the inner ward by Edward Herbert (d.1648), were ordered to be slighted. The castle was finally passed to the state in 1963.

• **Buildings** Approaching from the path, the visitor reaches a modern bridge over the first of two great ditches cut athwart the limestone ridge. Down on the right is the foundation of a seventeenth-century dovecot. Then one passes through the gatehouse into the middle ward, all originally of 1251–53; the many lesser walls within the defences belong to later periods, some relating to the house built here by Edward Herbert. The second ditch is crossed by a modern bridge into the original castle of 1224–30. This ditch had been filled in when the castle was abandoned, and its excavators found six hundred pieces of armour from the Civil War period.

Grooves for the portcullis can be seen in the passageway. This was where the widow Maud Vras ('stout Maud') was killed by a falling stone in 1288; the inquest on her reported that she had come from the town to recover her kettle. The massive inner gatehouse contained the main accommodation for the king when visiting, or his constable. On the left the well-tower; the well itself was cut to a depth of at least 60 metres (200 feet); the labour involved in raising water must have been exhausting. At the far end is the later kitchen and brewhouse. Surviving pieces of carved red ashlar dressing came from Shrewsbury, and some bear masons' marks. It is worthwhile to walk round the outside of the castle; from a lower standpoint the ruins are still impressive, as are the huge ditches which must have supplied much of the stone.

POWIS CASTLE

SJ 215 064. National Trust. Fee.

• **Access** Powis Castle and its gardens are one of the glories of Wales, to be found well-signposted off the A483 south of Welshpool (itself an attractive historic town). As you approach along the narrow road, pause if you can at the magnificent iron gates to enjoy one of the best views of the castle and gardens. The road then leads up through the park, where with luck deer may be seen, to the ticket office and parking ground. The buildings, gardens, Clive museum and catering make a full day at the castle a special experience. It is owned by the National Trust. This is the only castle of Welsh origin which remained a home throughout the medieval and modern periods. The spelling 'Powis' is an anglicism for Welsh 'Powys', the usual spelling of the Welsh principality and modern county.

• **History** There are two early mottes in the area, one at Welshpool, the other south-west of the castle. The first timber building on the present splendid site may have been the work of Owain Cyfeiliog (d.1197), warrior poet-prince of southern Powys, or more likely his fierce son Gwenwynwyn (d.1216). Gwenwynwyn's son Gruffudd maintained a long alliance with the English Crown which, together with his conspiracy against Llywelyn ap Gruffudd, ensured that the latter's wrath fell on the castle in 1274 and destroyed it. However, Gruffudd escaped, returned to the castle in 1277 and he and his lordship survived the Edwardian conquest. He may have begun the earliest stonework to survive. His granddaughter Hawys Gadarn ('the Strong'), took the castle and lordship by marriage to John de Charleton in 1309. In 1587 the castle was bought by Sir Edward Herbert, one of the great Herbert dynasty (see also Raglan), and he began the long process of turning a still-habitable fortress into a fine country home. Edward's son

The Red Castle of Powys.

William, the first Lord Powis, defended the castle for the king against parliament in 1644, but was forced to surrender. His son restored the damage of the Civil War, and his grandson William was made marquess of Powis in 1674, and when, being a loyal Catholic like his forefathers, he followed James II into exile in 1688, he was made Duke of Powis – the only Welsh duke ever. Local Protestant rioters ransacked the castle to express their disgust.

The duke's son, yet another William, rejected the dukedom, which of course was not officially recognised, and accepted the Protestant succession to the throne though himself still Catholic. He struggled fiercely and successfully to recover his castle and estates from William III's Dutch nephew William van Zuylesteyn, Earl of Rochford, only for the next generation to run out of male heirs. The 16-year-old heiress Barbara, the family's last Catholic, married her 48-year-old ninth cousin Henry Herbert, who had been made Earl of Powis. Their only son failed to marry, but their daughter Henrietta married Edward, son of Clive of India, created Earl of Powis. Their son changed his name to Herbert. In 1883 the Powis estates contained 60,000 acres worth £57,000 a year; by 1950 it had shrunk severely. The castle and gardens were bequeathed to the National Trust in 1952, and the family gave up its apartment in 1988. The castle, the estates and the Herberts deserve a full-length historical study.

• **Buildings** The castle is best viewed from the south, when its red sandstone walls above the great terraces fully justify its Welsh title *Castell Coch* – the Red Castle. Visitors enter the courtyard via the west gate, a brick replacement of 1668 for the stone gateway blown up by puritan assailants in the Civil War. Between the gate and the entrance to the castle proper is a huge lead figure of Fame on horseback by Andrew Carpenter. On the left is the accommodation for the NT shop and tearoom; above them the former ballroom, which now houses Indian memorabilia from the Clive collection. The outer wall of this north-west complex is late thirteenth century, as is the fine twin-towered entrance to the castle itself. The castle interior is fascinating; its high point is the late sixteenth century long gallery, but before that the visitor passes through the dining room and up the back stairs to the library and the fine drawing room. The magnificent main staircase can be viewed by visitors but not used. The state bedroom is off the long gallery. There are fine portraits and paintings, including one of the best Elizabethan miniatures anywhere (in the library, often missed by visitors), as well as Greek vases, Mary Queen of Scots' rosary and a good deal of military memorabilia. Visitors exit through the kitchens and a large collection of stuffed creatures. The gardens are beyond the purview of this book; they are breathtaking.

PEMBROKESHIRE

CAREW

SN 045 037. National Park. Fee.

• **Access** This splendid estuary castle can be reached from Haverfordwest via the A40 and A4075, or from the east by the A477. There is a convenient car park and level walk to the entrance, passing the great Carew cross, the finest early medieval cross in Wales, which commemorates the death of King Maredudd of Dyfed in 1035 and is described in the Cadw guidebook to Lamphey and Llawhaden. The castle ticket also gives entry to the remarkable tidal mill to the west – not to be missed. There is a shop and guidebook, and historical reenactments are performed at weekends. The castle is closed during the winter.

• **History** Excavation in the 1990s showed that the castle site had originally been fortified by a series of at least six defensive ramparts, with ditches cut into the rock, work

Carew Castle and mill pond.

that probably dates from the late Roman and early medieval period. Given other finds, it seems that the site had been occupied more or less continuously for well over a thousand years before the building of the first castle. The presence of King Maredudd's cross, still in its original position, and the important ecclesiastical site at Carew Cheriton a mile away, both indicate that this was no ordinary place. When Gerald de Barri, constable of Pembroke, replaced the rebellious Arnulf as Henry I's representative in west Wales, the king gave him as wife the royal mistress Nest, daughter of Rhys ap Tewdwr (d.1093), the last Welsh king of the south-west. Carew may have been her dowry, another possible indication that this had long been a royal site.

Gerald or his son William took advantage of the ancient site to build a castle of his own, mostly of timber but fronted by a small stone tower, now part of the east front. William took the surname de Carew, and descendants added to the castle in the late twelfth-century and started rebuilding it in the thirteenth and fourteenth centuries. The castle was never attacked by the Welsh, and the Carew family flourished, owning much land in Ireland. Eventually Sir Edmund Carew mortgaged the castle to Sir Rhys ap Thomas (d.1525), greatest of the Welsh supporters of Henry Tudor at his Bosworth victory over Richard III. In 1507 Sir Rhys celebrated what was to be the last great medieval tournament in Wales at Carew, the fifth centenary of which was celebrated in 2007 by another tournament, with real jousting.

Sir Rhys did much to remodel and extend the castle before his death; when his grandson and heir was executed at Henry VIII's command on a trumped-up accusation of treason, Carew passed to the Crown. In 1558 Sir John Perrot, one of queen Elizabeth's greatest courtiers, became governor of Carew, and before his death in 1592 when imprisoned in the Tower of

London he carried out yet more rebuilding, transforming it into a Renaissance palace (see p.39). Eventually the castle was returned to the Carew family and was reinforced during the Civil Wars. It changed hands between royalists and parliamentarians in 1643–44, was fiercely besieged by the latter in 1646 and the kitchen range destroyed. In 1686 the Carew family abandoned their castle and moved to England. Slow decay followed, and Turner was able to paint Carew as a splendidly romantic ruin. Carew family descendants still own Carew, having leased it to the Pembrokeshire Coast National Park in 1983.

• **Buildings** The ruins are an intriguing mixture of medieval and renaissance architecture, the former typified in the great towers and walls, the latter by the splendid Elizabethan windows with surviving or replaced tracery, frequently inserted in much older walls. The visitor approaches across the outer ward, cleared of medieval buildings and reaches the outer gatehouse (c. 1500), leading to the middle ward. On the left is the south-east tower; in front are fragments of Civil War walling, behind which is the east range, with gatehouse. To the right of the gatehouse are the old tower, chapel tower and the semicircular end of Sir John Perrot's north range. Entering the inner ward through its gatehouse, one is opposite another gateway into the great hall, with two splendid towers at either end. On the right is the north range, while nearer at hand is the splendid vaulted undercroft beneath the lesser hall. Part of the value of visiting the tidal mill is the magnificent waterfront view of the castle across the mill lagoon.

CILGERRAN

SN 195 431. National Trust. Fee.

• **Access** This splendid castle, not as well-known as it should be, can be reached from either Cardigan or Haverfordwest and Crymych to the south by turning eastwards on the A478 at the small settlement of Pen-y-bryn. Visitors coming from Carmarthen and Newcastle Emlyn on the A484 can follow signs from Llechryd. Cilgerran is perched high above the point where the little river Plysgog joins the Teifi gorge; few Welsh castles have a finer situation. Unfortunately there is no easy parking available in summertime, but the effort to find a place is well worthwhile. Cilgerran is a good example of a medieval borough which never flourished as such, but survived as a village with attractive walks round about. There is an Ogam/Latin inscribed stone in the parish churchyard, the memorial of Trenegussus, son of Macutrenus. Cadw guidebook.

• **History** Given its cliff-top position, one would suppose that the castle was hard to storm, but it had a chequered history. Unfortunately its origin is uncertain; it may have been the same as the castle of Cenarth Bychan, established in the commote (later lordship) of Cemais about 1108 by Gerald of Windsor, who was expanding Norman rule from Pembroke. We know that Cenarth Bychan had hardly been established when it was stormed by the dynamic but erratic Owain ap Cadwgan of Powys. His purpose was not to occupy the castle but to seize Gerald's beautiful wife Nest, daughter of the late king of south Wales, Rhys ap Tewdwr. The *Chronicle of the Princes* tells us with relish how Nest helped her husband escape down the toilet shaft (feasible, but disgusting) before being carried off with her three children by the lustful Owain, a crime which the cuckolded Gerald eventually avenged by killing Owain. The story may owe something to later imagination, but that

Cilgerran's towers, built by the Marshalls of Pembroke.
Crown copyright RCAHMW.

Nest was an exciting woman is beyond doubt.

Cilgerran appears under its own name as the home of Robert fitz Stephen, son of Nest by another of her lovers, the constable of Cardigan castle. In 1165 Rhys ap Gruffudd routed the Anglo-Normans of Ceredigion and Cemais and seized Cilgerran castle, capturing Robert. The following year the Normans of Pembroke twice besieged Cilgerran in vain. Rhys held the castle until his death in 1197, after which it become one of many bones of contention between his quarrelsome sons. English power began to increase, and in 1204 William Marshall the elder marched from Pembroke with a large army and swept the Welsh out. In 1215 however Llywelyn the Great led the princes of Powys and the south in a remarkable campaign, virtually clearing the region between Carmarthen and Cardigan, successfully storming nine castles, including Cilgerran, which Llywelyn awarded to Maelgwn ap Rhys.

He was the last Welshman to hold Cilgerran, which was recaptured in 1223 by William Marshall the younger, and he it was who began the massive stoneworks which survive today, continued by his brothers. English ownership was sorely tested in 1257, when Llywelyn ap Gruffudd swept through the area and defeated the English, but failed to expel the garrison. Thenceforward the castle has little history. The lordship became associated for many years with the lordship of Abergavenny. Cilgerran did not figure, as far as is known, in any of Edward I's three major campaigns in Wales (1277, 1282–83, 1294–95), but it may have been briefly occupied by the Welsh in the Glyndŵr rebellion. It does not figure in the Civil Wars, and fell into romantic decay, exploited by Richard Wilson and JMW Turner. It became state property in 1943.

• **Buildings** The twelfth-century castle of Gerald, Nest and Owain, if this was its site, is barely visible at all under the weight of later building. Since the site is defended on more than half its circuit by cliffs, only the southern side needed serious defences. The first castle was probably defended by the massive ditch still visible, which now divides the inner from the outer wards. When William Marshall began to strengthen the site a circuit of stone walls was built in local slate, dominated by the first (east) tower, not unlike the massive drum-keep at Pembroke. The 3-storey inner gatehouse was reached from the outer ward by a drawbridge over the ditch. Either William or (more likely) one of his younger brothers ran a stone wall right round the outer ward, complete with a ditch (now infilled) and an outer gatehouse. Part of this wall collapsed in 1863 when undermined by slate quarrying.

A second massive tower was erected on the site of the original gatehouse, on the line of the curtain wall, now much strengthened, and new gatehouses were created in the inner and outer walls. At some time after 1275 the north curtain walls were rebuilt, with latrines at the east end, and in the fourteenth century the north-east tower was added, whose remains now give amazing views up and down the Teifi gorge. The picturesque mansion opposite is Coedmor, in Ceredigion. The Teifi used to be navigable from Cardigan and the sea as far as Cilgerran, until carelessly discarded slate-quarry waste reduced its draught. Stone footings survive in both outer and inner wards which supported domestic buildings.

HAVERFORDWEST

SM 943 157. Council-owned. Open access.

• **Access** This castle dominates the centre of town and is easily reached from the Riverside car park, though the last part of the walk is steep. The ruins are a shell open at all hours and not well labelled. A pamphlet is available either from the Museum building (once the prison governor's house) or the county Record Office, housed in the old prison, built in 1820.

Haverfordwest Castle.

• **History** The first lord of Haverfordwest was Tancred, one of the Flemings who colonised this part of Wales at the beginning of the twelfth century, but the name, meaning 'heifers' ford', is English (*cf.* Hertford). The site commands the crossing of the Western Cleddau river. Tancred must have built a motte here of which nothing now survives. The castle and growing town survived Welsh incursions to welcome Henry II from Ireland in 1173 and Archbishop Baldwin's crusade in 1188. About that time building work in stone was begun.

In 1210 King John confiscated the castle, which he visited several times while travelling to and from Ireland, granting it to William Marshall, Earl of Pembroke. In 1217 Llywelyn the Great, as part of a highly successful campaign in the south, menaced Haverfordwest so seriously that the Bishop of St David's intervened to arrange a truce. In 1220 Llywelyn returned, incensed by the treachery of the Flemings, and burnt the town but did not take the castle. In 1257 Llywelyn ap Gruffudd campaigned in the south, but failed to take Haverfordwest.

After the conquest of 1282–83 Edward I and Queen Eleanor arrived here on their way to St David's on pilgrimage. Eleanor was so taken with the castle that she bought it and spent over £400 on improvements. It remained in Crown hands and was repaired from time to time, surviving the 1405 invasion of Glyndŵr's French allies, though once again the town was destroyed. Finally in the Civil Wars the castle changed hands between Crown and Parliament several times before its capture by parliamentarian forces in 1645 and its subsequent slighting by order of Cromwell.

• **Buildings** Entering the outer ward from the west, the visitor passes the old prison into the shell of the inner ward. There are foundations of the great hall and solar to the south and great chamber and pantry to the east. The curtain walls still rise to a great height, and it is hardly surprising, given the steep approaches from three sides, that this castle was one of the best defended in Wales.

LLAWHADEN

SN 013 176. Cadw. Open access.

• **Access** A signed northward turning off the A40 at Canaston Bridge leads to Llawhaden village; turn right at the T-junction. The castle comes into view and there is a very small car park followed by a short walk; it would be possible to take an elderly or disabled person to the gateway and then drive back to park. A joint guidebook to Llawhaden and the Bishop's Palace at nearby Lamphey (well worth a visit) can be bought at the latter site.

• **History**   It was probably Bernard, first Norman bishop of St David's, who built a ringwork castle at this dominant site on church-owned land, *c.*1130. Bishops as castle-builders may seem strange to modern eyes, but given charge for their lifetimes of extensive lands they had to protect and enhance the Church's prestige and landownership, as well as taking part in the defence of the south against the Welsh of the north. Church status did not however deter Rhys ap Gruffudd from capturing and razing the castle in 1193. Bishop Thomas Bek, a chief minister of the English Crown, had begun developing Llawhaden as a borough with a weekly market (where the car park now is), annual fairs and a hospital. The castle was rebuilt in stone following the Welsh destruction. By 1326, with 126 burgesses, Llawhaden was as large a town as Cardigan or Aberystwyth.

By the fourteenth century, fears of Welsh assault had dwindled but there was the possibility of French attack. Adam de Houghton, bishop from 1362 to 1389, redeveloped the castle

Llawhaden: more bark than bite.

on a fairly grand scale, though it was more of a palace than a fortress. It was briefly garrisoned against the Glyndŵr rebellion, but was not assaulted. Bishop Barlow (d.1568) sold off the lead and timber to provide his daughter with a dowry, one of his lesser acts of vandalism in west Wales, and that was that.

• **Buildings** The massive ditch and ramparts are still impressive, but the impact of the fifteenth-century gatehouse is lessened by its stagy appearance, since much of the rear of the building has collapsed, leaving it isolated on both sides. It is nevertheless interesting, especially for the use of a band of purple Caerbwdi stone from St David's. Although provided with the conventional 'murder holes', this frontage with its high arch and large upper windows was clearly intended to impress rather than defend. The gatehouse would have provided apartments for the constable of the castle; the bishop's own apartments are to the right, with the chapel and massive porth further on. Opposite the gatehouse is the large hall block, with undercroft still vaulted beneath the hall floor, and to the left is the late medieval bakehouse. The castle ditch is noteworthy for its large number of wild flowering plants.

MANORBIER

SO 064 978. Privately owned. Fee.

• **Access**   Delightful Manorbier is reached from either Pembroke or Tenby by the A4139, and turning off at the village signs. The castle is splendidly sited on a strong promontory below the village; parking (free in winter) is below the castle. There is a shop and guidebook. The castle is open daily to summer visitors.

• **History**   Odo de Barri was one of the conquerors of south-west Wales in the last years of the eleventh century, and was granted this site. His son William married Angharad, daughter of Gerald of Windsor and the Welsh princess Nest. Their son, another Gerald, became the greatest Latin author of his times, leaving in particular his remarkable account of his journey round Wales in 1188 with Archbishop Baldwin of Canterbury and his *Description of Wales*. His description of Manorbier is deservedly famous, claiming that 'in all the wide lands of Wales, Manorbier is by far the most pleasant.' On a sunny day he cannot be gainsaid.

Manorbier was garrisoned against Glyndŵr but apparently left alone by him and his French allies. It was again garrisoned for the king in 1643 but captured in 1645. Ownership of the castle had passed to the Crown *c.*1400, and in 1670 to Sir Erasmus Philipps of Picton, and it is still owned by a descendant of the Philipps family. In the 1880s it was leased to JR Cobb, restorer of Caldicot and Pembroke, who did a great deal to secure the fabric and built the modern house within the walls. Among famous twentieth-century visitors were George Bernard Shaw and Virginia Woolf.

• **Buildings**   Dramatic without, well-gardened within, Manorbier certainly justifies Gerald's opinion. The curtain

Manorbier Castle.

walls, now largely lacking their walkways, form an irregular heptagon linking two twelfth-century extremes, the old tower and the hall keep. The curtain walls and most of the other fabric is thirteenth century. Circulating clockwise, the visitor can enter the round tower by passing between the shop and JR Cobb's house, which can be rented; the tower offers splendid views. Beyond the house are the ruined barns (sixteenth century), then comes the chapel and crypt, the solar and the hall keep itself. Beyond the keep are the well and kitchen, and on to the north tower. The castle was well equipped with garderobes, including a two-seater. There are several fine fifteenth-/sixteenth- century chimneys.

NARBERTH

SN 110 144. Open access.

• **Access** Although not on a major routeway, the small and pleasant town of Narberth lies where three minor roads all join the A478 running from Tenby to Cardigan and beyond, and it overlooks the deep valley of a tributary of the Eastern Cleddau river. It can be reached from east or west by the A40, which lies just north of the town, or by rail on the Haverfordwest line; the station is a little east of the town centre. There is no car park.

• **History** Although Narberth castle stands high above its valley on military guard, its raison d'être may have been essentially unmilitary. Arberth was a commote in the pre-Norman administrative system, and the large hummock on

The bare bones of Narberth.

which the castle stands may have had major significance long before the building was raised. According to the story of Pwyll, Prince of Dyfed, in the Mabinogion, Arberth was a chief *llys* or court of the Prince, who rose one day 'and went to the summit of a knoll situated above the court called the Knoll of Arberth', where he was told he would either endure wounds or see a wonder. Some scholars have looked elsewhere for the knoll or mound of Arberth, but there is no reason to; the mound is a splendid one, and the Norman invaders might well have chosen it for its ancient prestige as well as its strategic position. The Normans regularly took over Welsh land units and developed them as discrete lordships; such was the case with Arberth, now Narberth. The little town became a borough, and is pleasant to walk around, with a tiny town hall and some good houses.

The castle first appears on record in 1116, when it was attacked and burnt by Gruffudd ap Rhys in one of his vain efforts to recover the kingdom ruled by his father, Rhys ap Tewdwr. It must have been rebuilt, because a century later it was again burnt, by Llywelyn the Great in 1215 and again by him in 1220. It survived these onslaughts, only to be burnt a fourth time in 1256 by Llywelyn ap Gruffudd. Although in parlous state by the early sixteenth century, it was apparently inhabited until 1677.

• **Buildings** Ten years ago Narberth might not have figured in a book such as this; it was unsigned and overgrown. However a recent programme of clearance and excavation has improved its appearance enormously. It is a small castle, roughly rectangular; three of its four corner towers survive in varying condition. A vaulted cellar survives on the east side. The stonework is of the thirteenth century. Numerous graves were discovered during the archaeological excavation; perhaps the site had been ecclesiastical in earlier times.

PEMBROKE

SM 982 016. Trust-owned. Fee.

• **Access** Pembroke is one of the greatest Welsh castles. Most visitors will come by car via the A477 and find themselves denied entry to the town's main street by its one-way system. Instead one turns left onto lower ground (the common), and the road runs parallel to the narrow limestone ridge on which the town stands. There are parking grounds here, free in winter, and signs for the castle, which massively dominates the far end of the ridge. It is easily reached on foot from the car park. Alternatively it lies a kilometre's walk from the railway station. The owning trust publishes a guidebook.

• **History** A stranger might be puzzled, looking at a map of Wales, by the importance of a castle tucked away in what might

Pembroke Castle.

seem an obscure corner of the country. Yet the great ridge seems to have been a centre of settlement for many ages. Stone tools show that the huge cave beneath the castle, the Wogan, was an ancient refuge; Roman coins have been found on the ridge itself. Soon after the Normans first attacked Wales, William I came to an understanding with Rhys ap Tewdwr, king of the south-west, that he should be left in peace, but with Rhys's death in 1093 the truce ended, and Roger de Montgomery, Earl of Shrewsbury, swept into the fallen kingdom. The speed with which he made for Pembroke suggests that it was already important; here or nearby may even have been the site of King Rhys ap Tewdwr's *llys* or court. Roger began building a castle immediately, but before the end of 1094 he was dead. His youngest son, Arnulf, inherited Pembroke and its lordship lands.

Arnulf established a priory at Monkton on the next ridge south of the castle (the church is still there), but had to spend time at his lands in Yorkshire and elsewhere. He appointed a steward responsible for Pembroke, Gerald de Windsor, who held the new castle against a Welsh siege in 1094. Arnulf was not a wise man; in 1102 he and his brother Robert revolted against King Henry I, and fled to Ireland, leaving the castle in the king's hands. Henry had taken as one of his mistresses Nest, the beautiful daughter of the dead Welsh King Rhys, and fathered a child by her. He then gave her in marriage to Gerald of Windsor, who held the castle for the king. His offspring, collectively known as the Geraldines, became a power in the land, especially in Ireland. While the king was still in direct charge he ensured the foundation of a borough close to the castle, complete with its own mint. Settlers were brought from Flanders and the west of England to replace the native population, and little England beyond Wales began to flourish.

Henry I's successor, Stephen, granted the lordship of Pembroke to Gilbert de Clare, whom he made earl of Pembroke. Gerald de Windsor's son William became Gilbert's deputy. In 1148 Gilbert died, and it was his son Richard, 'Strongbow', who eventually responded to a crisis in Ireland by launching the first Anglo-French invasion. His highhanded behaviour provoked the wrath of Henry II, who took his lands and Pembroke Castle from him. He regained royal favour, but died in 1176, and because he had no son living, his daughter and heiress Isabel became a ward of the Crown. At the age of 17 she and her lands were given to the 43-year-old William Marshall, who had risen from obscurity to become the greatest knight in the realm, and he was made earl of Pembroke. He was a great castle builder and improver, and he it was who began to turn Pembroke castle into one of the greatest in Britain. After his death in 1219 he was succeeded in turn by each of his five sons, not one of whom produced an heir. In 1220 Llywelyn the Great invaded the Pembroke lordship, but was paid £100 by the townsfolk not to besiege the borough and castle.

By the time that the last of William Marshall's sons died in 1245 the castle had assumed much of its present shape; the great keep, the inner and outer wards were all in place. The lordship passed to an unpopular French incomer, William de Valence, husband of Marshall's granddaughter Joan and uncle to King Edward I. He rebuilt the outer ward of the castle and created new domestic buildings and a chancery from which to administer his extensive lands, which included swathes of France and Ireland. After his death in 1296, his son Aylmer spent little time in Wales, though he ordered the building of Pembroke's town walls. Aylmer died heirless, and the castle's fortunes declined. It passed through numerous hands and its condition deteriorated, though it was twice garrisoned against French invasion, in 1378 (threatened) and 1405 (actual, when a French army came to support Owain Glyndŵr).

Pembroke's fortunes revived under Jasper Tudor, made earl of Pembroke by his half-brother King Henry VI in 1457, and he took Margaret Beaufort, the pregnant 13-year-old widow of his brother Edmund Tudor to Pembroke castle, where her baby was born. In the confusions of the Wars of the Roses, Lancastrian fortunes collapsed in 1471 and Jasper carried Henry to safety in Brittany. He had done much to rehabilitate the castle, and built a now-vanished house in the outer ward. With Jasper's departure the castle lost its significance; under the Tudor regime the lordship of Pembroke ceased as a unit, though the title of earl of Pembroke was revived more than once.

The castle saw one more burst of activity in the Civil Wars. Alone among Welsh towns, Pembroke borough declared for Parliament in 1642, and mayor John Poyer strengthened the castle. The war ended, but in 1648 John Poyer led disaffected and unpaid Parliamentarian soldiers in revolt. Oliver Cromwell, now a general but not yet Protector, arrived in May with an army and besieged town and castle for two months before Poyer and his allies surrendered and Poyer was shot. Sections of the town walls were demolished and the south-facing towers partially destroyed. Desolation was complete.

The uninhabitable ruins attracted Romantic artists; the castle was painted by Richard Wilson (see p.41), Paul Sandby and JMW Turner among many others. Some renovations were undertaken in the Victorian period by JR Cobb, restorer of Caldicot castle, but it was taken in hand seriously in 1928 by Major-General Sir Ivor Philipps of the Picton family. At his own expense he mounted a ten-year programme of restoration and some excavation; the destroyed towers were rebuilt, as was much of the hall. World War II put a stop to the work; instead, huts were erected in the outer ward for troops of the

Royal Fusiliers. The castle was placed in the ownership of an independent trust, which administers and maintains it to the highest standards without government aid.

• **Buildings** You approach the castle via the Barbican, designed to menace any unwelcome visitor, and pass through the great gatehouse into the outer ward, whose defensive walls are largely thirteenth century, like the gatehouse itself. There are connecting exhibition rooms on two floors of the twin gatehouse towers, and it is possible to walk within the walls to the Henry VII tower on the left, climb stairs and walk back along the parapet. Further to the left is the Monkton tower, with strange graffiti in one of its chambers. Stop before reaching the ruined inner gate, and you stand on the infilled site of the original great ditch which defended the first castle. The low wall which crosses the site marks the original much higher inner curtain wall. All the masonry is local carboniferous limestone.

Enter the inner ward, and most of what remains is the Marshall castle of the late twelfth and early thirteenth centuries. On the left a narrow hall, re-roofed in modern times, dovetails between the curtain wall and the foundations of the chapel. To the right is the great tower, the castle's most famous feature. Begun by William Marshall in 1204, it stands to its original height of 25 metres, comprised of five stories, mostly for domestic accommodation, crowned with its original domed roof, and having an accessible parapet. This gives a fine overview of the chancery building and the slightly smaller old hall and great hall. The old hall, perhaps the work of Richard Strongbow, cannot have pleased William de Valence, who added the only slightly larger great hall and a garderobe (toilet) block behind it. He completed these late thirteenth-century additions by building the chancery, which acted as administrative headquarters and main court for several centuries following.

From a doorway in the great hall it is possible to reach stairs down to the watergate, within the huge Wogan cavern, barred in by a late twelfth-century wall through which access was possible to the Pembroke river. The dungeon tower bulges towards the outer ward, but is accessed close to the great tower and was convenient for prisoners brought in from sentencing in the chancery. Most tower basements, often perceived by children as dungeons, were simply storage cellars, but like the one at Kidwelly, this is the genuine article, accessed only by trapdoor from the first floor.

Returning to the outer ward, on the left is St Anne's bastion, a fourteenth-century addition, now housing modern toilets and a refreshment room. Then comes the northgate tower and we are back at the gatehouse. The tarmac square was not originally a parade ground, simply the town tennis courts. Considerable sections of the town walls survive, some in good condition, as well as a number of the original towers.

PICTON

SN 011 134. Trust-managed. Fee.

• **Access** Picton's castle and wonderful gardens are reached from a southward turn off the A40 between Haverfordwest and Canaston Bridge. Current opening times are much improved on those of a few years ago: 1 April to 30 September, daily except Mondays (but open Bank Holidays) 10.30am–5.00pm. Admission is to the gardens; the castle is only open (for a small extra fee) for hourly guided tours 11.30am–3.30pm. Picton has its own useful website at www.pictoncastle.co.uk with information about weddings and corporate events. There is a café and shop.

• **History** Like the owners of Carew, the present owners of

Picton: the medieval walls much civilised by the Philipps family.

Picton can trace their descent to the castle's first builder, Sir John Wogan (*fl.* 1300), though since it has passed several times through an heiress, the family surname became Dwnn and from 1469 Philipps, long the foremost family in the county. The most distinguished head of the family was Sir John Philipps (d.1737), a foremost promoter of religious and charitable institutions, including the circulating schools through which his brother-in-law, Griffith Jones of Llanddowror, brought literacy to tens of thousands of the common people of Wales.

Picton may have been captured by Owain Glyndŵr's French allies during their invasion of 1405, when they occupied much of what is now Pembrokeshire. It was certainly involved in the Civil Wars; the royalist general Charles Gerard forced its surrender in 1645 but had to abandon the county after the king's defeat at Naseby, and Picton was retaken by parliamentarian forces in the same year. The family, though sympathetic to the Commonwealth, had no difficulty in surviving the Restoration of 1660 with their lands and influence intact; a century later their sympathies were Jacobite.

• **Buildings**   The original castle was a motte east of the present buildings, later used as a garden viewpoint. Wogan's stone castle of *c.*1300 is at the heart of the present complex building. It was a massive keep with four corner towers, lacking any ward or open area within, and having a gatehouse with its own towers. The plan resembles Irish rather than Welsh castles, not surprisingly, since the Wogans had vast estates in Ireland. The original entry was at what is now the basement level, which suggests that, without a ditch or drawbridge, the castle was not military in purpose. The massive south-west tower now contains a splendid library, and thence the tour takes in the magnificent hall, dining room and ruggedly-vaulted undercroft. Picton is a castle outside, a stately home inside, with paintings and furniture of the highest quality. As such it bears comparison with the two other great castle-homes of Wales, Powis and Chirk. The gardens are a treat.

TENBY

SN 138 005. Open access.

• **Access**   Since little is left of Tenby's castle, and since the town is in summer quite overwhelmed with visitors, it may seem odd to include this castle in the catalogue of best Welsh castles at all. However, a fine winter's day makes parking possible at one of numerous small sites (better to come by train in the summer) and your visit will be amply repaid. If you are a stranger to the town, and park on the esplanade overlooking the wonderful south beach, you may be persuaded that the substantial fortification on St Catherine's Island is Tenby's castle. Not true – this is a 'Palmerston castle' of the 1860s, and though the island can be reached at low tide, the fort is inaccessible. Instead you will be struck by the medieval town wall, which is more impressive than the remaining stumpy tower on Castle Hill, which divides the south beach from the north.

The stump of Tenby's surviving tower.

• **History**   An unknown Norman built the first castle here, which was captured in 1156 by the Lord Rhys; his son Maelgwn sacked the town in 1187, and Llywelyn ap Gruffudd in 1260. Eventually walls were provided by William de Valence, which saved the town from being sacked by Owain Glyndŵr's French allies in 1405. Unusually for Pembrokeshire, the town declared for Charles I in the uprising of 1648, only to be taken by Cromwell.

• **Buildings**   Most of the town walls survive thanks to a Dr Chater, who succeeded in 1873 in preventing the town council from pulling it all down. They are less substantial than the royal walls of Caernarfon and Conwy, which are wide enough to carry walkways, and probably the vanished walls of most Welsh boroughs were on this scale. Of the castle only the stump of a gate tower, part of the barbican and a small tower which looks like conjoined twins, marrying a square and a round tower in one structure.

WISTON

SN 022 181. Open access.

• **Access** This is a surprisingly attractive site, despite the difficulties of approach caused by the inconspicuous and sometimes completely absent road-signs. Park by Wiston church and there beyond the hedge is the broad castle site, accessed either over a dangerous stile or by stepping cautiously across a cattle-grid. It's worth the effort.

• **History and site.** A massive Iron Age enclosure, with splendid bank and ditch all round, was seized upon by Wizo the Fleming (d.1130; from him the village takes its name) as the place for a large motte straddling the enclosure bank and ditch, which formed a huge bailey occupied by a medieval borough. He had been given the lordship of Daugleddau

Wiston motte and keep with its Iron Age defences.

about 1100. The motte, now reached by a flight of 46 steps, was later crowned by a small shell-keep. The Welsh stormed the castle in 1147, again in 1193, when Hywel Sais captured Philip fitz Wizo and his family, and yet again when Llywelyn the Great seized it in 1220. After that the castle was abandoned in favour of Picton, and at some stage the infant borough moved to the present village site. Wiston retains the classic medieval settlement pattern of castle, manor farm, church and civilian settlement. The ruin may have been a staging post for parliamentarian forces when they defeated a royalist army in 1645 at Colby Moor, between Wiston and Llawhaden.

RADNORSHIRE

NEW RADNOR

SO 216610. Footpath access.

• **Access** The medieval borough of New Radnor and its castle are easily accessible from the A44, west of Kington, east of Llandegly. Parking in the quiet streets is easy, and a public footpath just east of a house called The Forge gives access to the castle site. Although the walk is brief, the scramble up the castle mound is steep and shaggy with thick grass. From the top it is easy to make out the borough's medieval earthen ramparts, and the strategic value of the castle site, dominating its valley, is clear. Tiny though it has always been, New Radnor enjoyed borough status until 1833. Although no stonework remains, and although the plan of the castle is baffling, the site itself is well worth a visit. Disappointingly the medieval church was replaced by a Victorian nonentity; for a great church, go to Old Radnor, east down the A44 and up the hill right.

New Radnor Castle and borough walls from the air.
Crown copyright RCAHMW.

• **History** The castle's history is as complex and problem-ridden as is understanding its remains, which have been variously described as a motte-and-bailey and a ringwork-and-bailey by different authorities. It may have been started as early as 1070 by William fitz Osbern. It may have become a Braose castle as early as 1096, part of the Braose mini-empire in eastern Wales. It was destroyed by Rhys ap Gruffudd in 1196 on his last ferocious onslaught in mid-Wales. By 1215 it was certainly a Braose castle. It was taken by Llywelyn the Great on his great sweep through mid-Wales in 1231 following his hanging of William de Braose for making him a cuckold. Rebuilt by the Earl of Cornwall, it was again taken by Llywelyn ap Gruffudd in 1264 late in his dramatic rise to power over more than two-thirds of Wales. It is clear from the careers of the two Llywelyns that they saw control of eastern mid-Wales as essential to their designs. Rebuilt in stone by Edward Mortimer after 1262, it was garrisoned against the Welsh in the war of 1282–83 and stormed by Owain Glyndŵr in 1402. On that occasion sixty men of the garrison were slaughtered; their decapitated skeletons came to light in 1845.

Description. The massive mound which the public footpath skirts is part natural, part artificial. Its flat summit is fifty yards across, surrounded with ramparts which explain why at least one historian has called it a ringwork, though it is difficult to agree. The original entrance is clearly visible, with what must be the foundations of a tower on one side. West of the mound is a large bailey. Nothing remains of Mortimer's stonework, probably robbed out to build houses. The complexities of the site will only become clear if or when it is excavated.

PAINSCASTLE

SO 166 462. Permission needed.

• **Access** Painscastle is beneath the interest of the Cadw guidebook to Clwyd and Powys, which is a pity, because this is an awesome set of earthworks with a complex history. Painscastle village, which it is difficult to believe was once a borough, can best be reached either by turning off the A470 onto the B4594 north of Erwood or from the A44 west of Kington. The quiet and attractive village has plenty of space for parking; best to enquire at the Roast Ox inn to find the house where permission for access can be had, only 200 yards away.

• **History** Sitting on the giant motte in September sunshine, contemplating the lovely green view westward, I found it difficult to believe that the *cantref* of Elfael, of which Painscastle was the centre, had been a district of frequent warfare between the local Welsh dynasty and its neighbours. The village is named for Pain fitzJohn, a royal chamberlain and major English landowner in the early twelfth century, for whom Painswick (Glos.) is also named. Little is known of his Welsh activities, but if he built this castle he did not enjoy it long; the Welsh killed him in 1137, and the castle became the property of the native prince of Elfael, Madog ab Idnerth. Comparative peace prevailed for a while, but about 1195 William de Braose, Lord of Brecon, took the castle and strengthened it.

The castle survived attack by Rhys ap Gruffudd in 1196, and again in 1198 when besieged by Gwenwynwyn, prince of southern Powys. King John seized it from William de Braose in 1208, but in 1215, when John was eating humble pie at the hands of the English barons and Llywelyn the Great, the local prince Gwallter ab Einion Clud took over the castle and held it until his death, when it passed into Llywelyn's hands. Henry III retook the site in 1231 and made it a castle of stone, granting it to Roger Tosny. This, along with his new castle at Montgomery, was part of Henry's strategy to strengthen the English frontier, but Llywelyn stormed and destroyed the castle in 1265. Rebuilt in 1277 by Ralph Tosny after Llywelyn's defeat by Edward, the castle remained defensible during Glyndŵr's revolt, but then fades from history.

Earthworks. Painscastle is not unlike Builth castle, a once proud stone fortress whose masonry has virtually disappeared,

The mighty earthworks of Painscastle.

leaving a hugely complex set of earthworks. The two most striking features are the motte, which like the surrounding moat and ditches, is massive, and the castle plan, which is rectangular. The motte is at the south end of the complex, splendidly ditched about, with a large bailey to the north and a barbican entrance on the west. Fragments of Roman work have led to speculation that the rectangle was once a Roman fort, but guesswork without excavation is vain.

APPENDIX A

MEDIEVAL CASTLES IN
WALES: A LIST

This is a rash venture, since it is most unlikely that any two students of Welsh castles would produce identical lists; even the best authorities cannot always agree whether a site can be defined as a castle or not. For all counties except Glamorgan, the list is based on DJC King's magisterial *Castellarium Anglicanum* (London, New York 1983), and checked for all counties with the Royal Commission's COFLEIN website, which is rather more conservative than DJC King. For Glamorgan's castles I have used the Royal Commission's splendid inventories. Choosing between such authorities is difficult, to say the least. John Wiles of the Royal Commission has kindly discussed the matter with me. He points out the difficulties of identification both of the nature and period of any given site, not least where it is possible that a motte may have been hastily thrown up and as hastily abandoned.

In its caution COFLEIN sometimes describes a site as of unknown date, or of being 'Medieval'. Sometimes it prefers to 'motte' or 'ringwork' the vaguer terms 'mound' or 'defended enclosure'. Some of these sites are to be found in a secondary list below of Lost, Post-medieval or Possible Castles, others I have ventured to include in the main list on the authority of DJC King. Some minor castles have been lost due to later urban or agricultural development, and their sites can no longer be identified with certainty. Some sites are known but even the nature of the castle is uncertain. Others are later, vanity buildings, which appear either in Appendix B or not at all. Some buildings known by the name of castle were in fact manor houses, or, mostly in Pembrokeshire, tower houses; some of these have been included in the secondary lists. Many such judgements are bound to be subjective.

Orthography. Many castles have more than one name; in most cases I have used the name favoured by the Royal Commission, usually in the current Ordnance Survey spelling, modified where necessary by Elwyn Davies's standard *Gazetteer of Welsh Place-Names* (Cardiff, many reprints). It is a pity that the Commission has not always adopted that guide, nor has the Ordnance Survey always done so. Anyone searching for place-names in COFLEIN may find it necessary to experiment with names such as Castell y Rhingyll (to be found in COFLEIN as *Castellrhingyll*), with compound names sometimes hyphenated, sometimes not. Where alternative names exist, they are included occasionally in the first column of names, more usually in the last. Castles known by the name *Domen* (a mound) are listed under *Tomen*, the unlenited form. Some castles are known by the Welsh prefix *Castell* + qualifier; such sites may appear in the list either as *Castell* + *X* or simply as *X*. It would have been impracticable to give every alias a separate line.

It was the original intention to note in every case whether sites have public access or are on private land, and if so whether visible or not from public land, or are open to the public by admission payment. This proved quite impossible to achieve when dealing with over three hundred sites. Most lesser sites are on private land and permission to visit them should be sought. To enable ready location of each site, its government Community name is in parentheses in the Notes; these names are now in use on all recent OS maps. There is an admitted drawback to this usage, since well-known villages are sometimes subsumed in less familiar names; thus Castell Gwallter, close to the village of Llandre, Cardiganshire, is in the community of Genau'r-glyn. Other community names are quite unexpected (Newport Gwent is in the community of Stow Hill) or lengthy (e.g. 'St David's and the Cathedral Close').

Column 1. * Indicates a castle described in the text, with details of access with page number in brackets after name.

Column 2. M = Earth Motte R = Ringwork S = Stone. This usage can be problematic; Cardiff has both a motte, a later stone keep on it, and further developments. For the sake of simplicity, if there is stonework, then 'S' is the definition. If there was stonework now vanished E = Earthworks may be used.

Column 3 gives the National Grid reference.

Column 4. This column, necessarily laconic, gives community names and alternative castle names, whether a fee is payable, and whether a castle is now a private home. There are also indications where a castle has nearly disappeared but is still identifiable. I have also noted with a 'W' those castles which were, or are highly likely to have been, founded by Welsh princes, even if the visible remains are English. These are not the judgements of the Royal Commission, but depend on DJC King and other authorities cited in the introduction. Where a degree of uncertainty is expressed I have cited either 'King' or 'RC' (for Royal Commission). As explained above, the community location are given in parentheses in their official spelling. I have referred when space allowed to the castle's siting within an Iron Age or Roman fort.

Anglesey

Name		Grid	Notes
Aberlleiniog	M	SH 616 794	*Llangoed*
*Beaumaris (45)	S	SH 607 763	*Beaumaris*
Castell Bryn Gwyn	R	SH 465 670	*Llanidan; 'multiperiod' RC*
Llanfaethlu	R	SH 291 859	*Cylch-y-garn; uncertain RC*

Breconshire

Castle Name		Grid	Notes
Aberllynfi	M	SO 171 380	*Gwernyfed*
Aberysgir	M	SO 000 295	*Yscir; RC is doubtful*
Alexanderstone	M	SO 073 300	*Llanddew*
Blaenllynfi	S	SO 145 229	*Llanfihangel Cwmdu*
Boughrood	E	SO 132 391	*Glasbury*
*Brecon I (47)	S	SO 044 286	*Brecon; part hotel, part private*
Brecon II	M	SO 070 295	*Brecon*
*Bronllys (49)	S	SO 149 346	*Bronllys*
*Builth (50)	S	SO 044 510	*Builth*
Bwlch y Ddinas	S	SO 179 301	*Talgarth; highest site in E. & W.*
Caer Beris	M	SO 029 507	*Cilmery aka Llanganten*
Carnycastell	M	SO 158 297	*Talgarth; almost ploughed out*
Castell Coch	S	SN 936 145	*Ystradfellte*
Castell Du	S	SN 919 284	*Maescar[4] W*
Cilwhybert	M	SO 014 268	*Glyn Tarell; aka Modrydd*
Crickadarn	R[5]	SO 059 412	*Erwood*

*Crickhowell I (53)	S	SO 217 182	*Crickhowell*
Crickhowell II	M	SO 206 195	*Crickhowell*
Cwm Camlais	S	SN 956 261	*Trallong; many aliases; W*
*Hay-on-Wye I (54)	S	SO 229 423	*Hay*
Hay-on-Wye II	M	SO 226 422	*Hay*
Hen Gastell Llangattock	S	SO 213 166	*Llangattock*
Llandefaelog-fach	M	SO 033 323	*Honddu Isaf*
Llanthomas	M	SO 209 403	*Llanigon*
Madog's Castle I	R	SO 025 370	*Honddu Isaf*
Madog's Castle II	M	SO 024 369	*Honddu Isaf*
Pencelli	S	SO 095 249	*Talybont-on-Usk*
Pen-llys	R	SN 998 584	*Llanafan Fawr; aka Llysdinam*
Pont Estyll	R	SO 009 270	*Glyn Tarell*
Trecastle	M	SN 882 292	*Llywel*
Tredustan	M	SO 140 324	*Talgarth*
Trefecca I	R	SO 145 314	*Talgarth; badly damaged*
Trefecca II	M	SO 142 323	*Talgarth; Badly damaged*
*Tretower[6] (56)	S	SO 184 212	*Llanfihangel Cwmdu*
Twdin I		SN 922 501	*Treflys; aka Treflis King*
Twdin II	R	SN 919 520	*Treflys aka Llanlleonfel*
Twmpan	M	SO 125 256	*Llangors*

Caernarfonshire

Castle Name		Grid	Notes
Aber	M	SH 656 727	*Aber; aka Y Mwd*
Bryn Castell	M	SH 785 719	*Caerhun; aka Tal-y-cafn*
*Caernarfon (59)	S	SH 477 627	*Caernarfon*
Carn Fadrun	S	SH 278 352	*Tudweiliog; W, within hillfort*
*Conwy (63)	S	SH 784 755	*Conwy*
*Cricieth (67)	S	SH 500 377	*Cricieth; W*
*Deganwy (64)	S	SH 781 794	*Conwy; W origin*
Dinas Emrys	S	SH 606 492	*Beddgelert; W*
*Dolbadarn (69)	S	SH 586 598	*Llanberis; W*
Dolbenmaen	M	SH 506 430	*Dolbenmaen; possibly W*
*Dolwyddelan (71)	S	SH 722 523	*Dolwyddelan; W*
Llannor	M	SH 346 382	*Llannor; aka Y Mount*
Llanystumdwy	R	SH 454 377	*Llanystumdwy; aka Tomen Fawr*
Tomen Castell	S?	SH 724 521	*Dolwyddelan*

Cardiganshire

Castle Name		Grid	Notes
*Aberystwyth I (75)	R	SN 584 790	*Llanfarian; aka Old Aberystwyth*
*Aberystwyth II (74)	S	SN 579 816	*Aberystwyth*
Adpar	M	SN 309 409	*Llandyfriog. Not on OS Landranger*
Blaen-porth	M	SN 266 488	*Aberporth; aka Castell Gwithian*

*Caer Pen-rhos (79)	R	SN 552 695	*Llanrhystud*
Caerwedros	M	SN 376 557	*Llandysiliogogo*
*Cardigan I (77)	S	SN 177 459	*Cardigan; restoration in progress*
Cardigan II	M	SN 164 464	*Cardigan; aka Old Castle*
Castell Gwallter	M	SN 623 868	*Genau'r-glyn*
Castell Gwynionydd[7]	R	SN 424 420	*Llandysul*
Castell Hywel/ Wmffre	M	SN 440 476	*Llandysul*
Castell Nantygaran	M	SN 370 421	*Llandyfriog*
Castell Pistog	M	SN 382 403	*Trefeurig aka Bangor*
Castell Pant- mawr	R	SN 611 756	*Llanilar; aka Coed y Castell*
Dinerth	M	SN 495 624	*Dyffryn Arth; complex earthworks*
Lampeter	M	SN 579 695	*Lampeter*
Llanfair Treflygan	M	SN 344 442	*Llandyfriog; aka St Mary's*
Llandyfriog	R	SN 351 411	*Llandyfriog*
Llanio	M	SN 661 579	*Llanddewibrefi*
Llanwnnen	M	SN 500 472	*Llanwnnen; aka Castell Du*
Llwyndyrys	M	SN 237 433	*Beulah; aka Henllys, Llandygwydd*
Llwyn Gwinau	M	SN 669 634	*Tregaron*
Nantygaran	M	SN 369 421	*Llandyfriog; aka Penrhiwllan*
Parcycastell	M	SN 288 427	*Beulah*

Peithyll	M	SN 653 823	*Trefeurig*
Penycastell	R	SN 630 746	*Llanilar; modified Iron Age fort[8]*
Rhydowen	M	SN 444 447	*Llandysul*
Tomen Las (Glandyfi)[9]	M	SN 687 968	*Ysgubor-y-coed; aka Aberdyfi*
* Trefilan (79)	M	SN 549 571	*Nantcwnlle; W*
Ystrad Meurig I	M	SN 718 678	*Ystrad Meurig*
Ystrad Meurig II	S	SN 702 675	*Ystrad Meurig; aka Cwm Meurig*

Carmarthenshire

Castle Name		Grid	Notes
Aber Taf	R	SN 297 136	*St Clears; aka Aber Carwy*
Banc Llwyndomen	M	SN 585 033	*Llanedi; aka Hendy, Ystum Enlli*
Banc y Bettws	M	SN 458 155	*Llangyndeyrn*
Carmarthen (81)	S	SN 413 200	*Carmarthen*
*Carreg Cennen (83)	S	SN 668 191	*Dyffryn Cennen; W*
Castell Du	M	SN 437 341	*Llanfihangel-ar-Arth*
Castell Nonni	M	SN 495 399	*Llanllwni; aka Castell Prysg*
Castell y Domen	M	SN 436 125	*Llangyndeyrn*
*Dinefwr (86)	S	SN 611 218	*Llandeilo W*
Dinweilir	M	SN 522 233	*Llanegwad; aka Allt-y-Ferin[10]*
*Dryslwyn (89)	S	SN 554 203	*Llangathen; W*
Egremont	R	SN 094 202	*Clynderwen*
Glan Mynys	M	SN 731 326	*Llanwrda*

Gwyddgrug	M	SN 477 356	*Llanfihangel-ar-Arth*
Hendy Motte	M	SN 584 032	*Llanedi*
*Kidwelly (91)	S	SN 409 070	*Kidwelly*
*Laugharne (95)	S	SN 303 107	*Laugharne Township*
Llanboidy	M	SN 219 231	*Llanboidy*
*Llandovery (98)	S	SN 767 343	*Llandovery*
Llanddowror	M	SN 253 147	*Llanddowror*
Llangadog	M	SN 709 276	*Llangadog aka Castell Meurig*
Llanllwni	M	SN 474 413	*Llanllwni*
*Llansteffan (100)	S	SN 351 101	*Llansteffan; within hillfort*
Llanwinio	M	SN 247 275	*Llanwinio aka Castell Bach*
Llwynbedw	M	SN 431 397	*Llanfihangel-ar-Arth*
*Newcastle Emlyn (102)	S	SN 311 407	*Newcastle Emlyn W*
Newchurch	R	SN 396 238	*Newchurch & Merthyr; aka Garn Fawr*
Parcydomen	M	SN 269 414	*Cenarth; aka Domen Fawr*
Pencader	M	SN 444 362	*Llanfihangel-ar-Arth*
Pencastell	M	SN 402 379	*Llangeler; aka Castell Mair*
Pen-y-cnap	M	SN 516 213	*Llanegwad*
St Clears	M	SN 281 154	*St Clears; aka Bancybeili*
Talley	M	SN 631 334	*Talley*
Tir-y-dail	M	SN 624 125	*Ammanford; ?W*
Tomen Lawddog	M	SN 360 362	*Llangeler; aka Pen-boyr*
Tomen Seba	M	SN 325 370	*Llangeler; aka Bwlch y Domen*
Waun Twmpath	M	SN 466 026	*Cefn Sidan*

Denbighshire

Castle Name		Grid	Notes
*Chirk Castle (104)	S	SJ 268 381	*Chirk; National Trust*
Chirk Motte	M	SJ 291 376	*Chirk*
*Denbigh (106)	S	SJ 051 657	*Denbigh*
*Dinas Bran (110)	S	SJ 222 430	*Llangollen*
Erddig	M	SJ 327 487	*Marchwiel*
Holt	S	SJ 411 537	*Holt*
Llangwm	M	SJ 012 445	*Llangwm Conwy*
Llys Gwenllian	M	SJ 056 643	*Denbigh[11]*
Pentrefoelas	M	SH 870 522	*Pentrefoelas*
*Ruthin (112)	S	SJ 124 579	*Ruthin*
*Sycharth (115)	M	SJ 205 258	*Llansilin; court of Owain Glyndŵr*
Tomen Cefn Glaniwrch	M	SJ 148 253	*Llanrhaeadr-ym-Mochnant*
Tomen Pentre Isaf	M	SH 874 688	*Llangernyw*
*Tomen y Faerdre (116)	M	SJ 193 561	*Llanarmon-yn-Iâl*
Tomen y Maerdy	M	SJ 148 239	*Llanrhaeadr-ym-Mochnant*
*Tomen y Rhodwydd (116)	M	SJ 176 516	*Llandegla; W*

Flintshire

Castle Name		Grid	Notes
Bryn-y-Cwn	M	SJ 238 714	*Flint; RC spells 'Bryn-y-cwm'*
*Caergwrle (118)	S	SJ 307 572	*Hope; aka Hope; W*
Dyserth	S	SJ 060 799	*Dyserth/Diserth*
*Ewloe (120)	S	SJ 288 675	*Hawarden; W*
*Flint (123)	S	SJ 247 733	*Flint*
*Hawarden (126)	S	SJ 319 654	*Hawarden*
Hen Blas	S	SJ 221 734	*Bagillt; aka Coleshill Castle*
Holywell	M	SJ 185 763	*Holywell; aka Basingwerk*
Leeswood[12]	M	SJ 235 644	*Leeswood*
Mold	M	SJ 235 644	*Mold; aka Bailey Hill*
Mount Cop	M	SJ 470 409	*Bronington*
Prestatyn	M	SJ 072 833	*Prestatyn*
*Rhuddlan (128)	S	SJ 024 779	*Rhuddlan*
Trueman's Hill	M	SJ 312 659	*Hawarden*
Twthill	M	SJ 026 777	*Rhuddlan*
Tyddyn Mount	M	SJ 252 632	*Mynydd Isa*

Glamorgan

Castle Name		Grid	Notes
Barry	S	ST 101 672	*Barry*
Bishopston	M	SS 582 900	*Bishopston; aka Barland*
Bonvilston	R	ST 071 734	*St Nicholas & Bonvilston*
Brynwell	R	ST 147 744	*Michaelston; aka Beganston*
Cae Castell I	E	ST 210 789	*Rumney*
Cae Castell II	R	ST 226 803	*Rumney*

Caerau	R	ST 136 750	*Caerau; within hill-fort*
*Caerphilly (131)	S	ST 155 871	*Caerphilly*
*Cardiff (135)	S	ST 180 767	*Castle Cardiff; within Roman fort*
Castell Bolan	M	SS 767 920	*Cwmafon; aka Cwm Clais; ?W*
*Castell Coch (139)	S	ST 131 826	*Tongwynlais*
Castell Nos	E	SS 966 001	*Aberdare; W*
Coed-y-cwm	E	ST 177 689	*St Nicholas & Bonvilston*
*Coety (141)	S	SS 923 815	*Coity Higher*
Cottrell	M	ST 080 745	*St Nicholas & Bonvilston*
Dinas Powys I	S	ST 152 716	*Dinas Powys*
Dinas Powys II[13]	R	ST 148 722	*Dinas Powys*
Felin Isaf	M	ST 061 793	*Pendoylan*
*Fonmon (144)	S	ST 047 681	*Rhoose; private home*
Gelli-garn	R	SS 960 787	*Llangan*
Gwern-y-domen	R	ST 175 878	*Van; aka Tomen Bedwas*
Howe Mill	R	SS 942 732	*Llandow; barely recognisable on ground*
Kenfig	S	SS 801 826	*Cynffig*
Llanblethian	S	SS 989 742	*Cowbridge with Llanblethian*
Llangynwyd	S	SS 852 887	*Llangynwyd Middle*
Llanilid	R	SS 977 813	*Llanharan*
Llanquian	S	ST 032 745	*Cowbridge with Llanblethian*
Llantrisant	S	ST 047 834	*Llantrisant*
Llantrithyd	R	SS 045 727	*Llancarfan*
*Loughor (147)	S	SS 564 980	*Llwchwr; within Roman fort*
Morganstown	M	ST 128 818	*Radyr*

Morgraig	S	ST 160 843	Caerphilly; W[14]
*Morlais (149)	S	SO 048 097	Pant
Neath	S	SS 753 978	Neath
*Newcastle (151)	S	SS 902 801	Bridgend
*Ogmore (153)	S	SS 882 769	St Brides Major
*Oxwich (146)	S	SS 497 862	Penrice; Tudor mansion on castle site
*Oystermouth (155)	S	SS 613 883	Mumbles
Pancross	R	ST 046 700	Llancarfan
Penllyn Castle	S	SS 988 761	Penllyn
Penlle'r Castell	S	SS 664 094	Mawr
Penmaen	R	SS 534 882	Ilston
Penmark	S	ST 059 689	Rhoose
*Pennard (145)	S	SS 544 885	Pennard
Penrice I	M	SS 497 887	Penrice; aka Mountybank
*Penrice II (147)	S	SS 498 885	Penrice
Pen-y-Pîl	R	ST 226 803	Rumney
Peterston	S	ST 084 764	Peterston
Ruperra	M	ST 223 867	Rudry; built 1626
*St Donat's (157)	S	SS 935 681	St Donat's; used by Atlantic College
St Fagan's	S	ST 120 772	St Fagans; largely rebuilt 16th/17th century
St Nicholas Gaer	R	ST 084 748	Peterston
St Quintin's	S	S	SS 985 791
Stormy	M	SS 847 815	Cynffig
*Swansea (160)	S	SS 657 931	Castle Swansea

240

Tal-y-bont	M	SN 586 026	*Grovesend; aka Hugh's Castle, Castell Du*
Tal-y-fan	S	ST 021 772	*W St Donats*
Tomen-y-clawdd	M	ST 091 864	*Llantwit Faerdre; aka Coed-y-tŵr*
Twmpath Motte	M	ST 154 822	*Rhiwbina; aka Caer Cynwrig*
Twyn	M	ST 137 969	*Gelli-gaer; aka Gelli-gaer; W*
Walterston	E	ST 068 712	*Llancarfan*
*Weobley (147)	S	SS 478 928	*Llanrhidian Lower*
Ynys-crug	M	SS 994 927	*Trealaw; aka Hangman's Hill*
Ystradowen	M	ST 011 777	*Penllyn; 'an uncompleted motte' RC*

Merionethshire

Castle Name		Grid	Notes
Carndochan	S	SH 846 306	*Llanuwchllyn; W*
*Castell y Bere (162)	S	SH 667 085	*Llanfihangel-y-Pennant; W*
Castell Cynfal	M	SH 615 016	*Bryncrug; aka Brynycastell; ?W*
Castell Gronw	M	SH 930 350	*Llangywer*
Corwen	M	SJ 056 438	*Corwen*
Crogen	M	SJ 005 370	*Llandderfel; ?W*
Cwm Prysor	S	SH 758 369	*Trawsfynydd; ?W*
Deudraeth	M	SH 588 371	*Penrhyndeudraeth; aka Gwaun Goch*
*Harlech (164)	S	SH 581 312	*Harlech*
Hendom	M	SJ 056 430	*Corwen*

Owain Glyndŵr's Mount	M	SD 125 431	*Corwen*
Penucha'r Llan	R	SH 938 368	*Llandderfel; aka Llanfor*
Tomen Ddreiniog	M	SH 597 036	*Llanegryn; W*
Tomen Las	M	SH 697 002	*Pennal*
*Tomen-y-mur (167)	M	SH 705 386	*Maentwrog*
Tomen y Bala	M	SH 928 360	*Bala*

Monmouthshire

Castle Name		Grid	Notes
*Abergavenny (168)	S	SO 299 139	*Abergavenny*
Berries, The	M[15]	ST 488 895	*Caldicot; aka Ballan Mount; Crick*
Bowling Green Llangibby	R	ST 369 973	*Llangybi*
Caerleon	S	ST 342 905	*Caerleon*
Caerwent	M	ST 471 903	*Caerwent*
*Caldicot (170)	S	ST 488 886	*Caldicot*
Castell Glas	M	ST 301 858	*Gaer*
Castle Arnold	E	SO 320 100	*Llanover[16]*
Castell Meredydd	S	ST 226 887	*Graig; aka Machen; W*
Castell Taliorum	M	ST 216 022	*Llanhilleth; aka Castell Tal-y-rhiw*
Castell Troggy	S	ST 415 952	*Shirenewton*
*Chepstow (172)	S	ST 533 941	*Chepstow*

Cwrt-y-gaer	R	ST 449 999	*Devauden; aka Wolves Newton*
Dingestow	E	SO 455 104	*Mitchel Troy*
Dinham	S	ST 480 923	*Llanbadoc*
Dixton	M	SO 521 135	*Monmouth*
*Grosmont (180)	S	SO 405 244	*Grosmont*
Graig Foel	R	SO 369 010	*Llanbadoc; 'ring-motte' RC*
Gwern Castle	M	SO 353 233	*Grosmont*
Kemeys Inferior	M	ST 389 935	*Langstone; aka Gipsies Mount*
Langstone Court	M	ST 371 895	*Langstone*
Llanfair Discoed	S	ST 446 923	*Caerwent*
Llanfair Kilgeddin	M	SO 349 069	*Langstone*
Llangwm	R	ST 427 997	*Llangwm*
Llangybi	S	ST 364 974	*Llangybi; 14th century*
Llantarnam[17]	M	ST 319 924	*Caerleon; aka Craig yr Eurych*
Mill Wood	M	SO 460 104	*Mitchel Troy*
Monmouth	S	SO 507 129	*Monmouth*
Newcastle	M	SO 447 172	*Llangattock-vibon-avel*
*Newport (175)	S	ST 312 885	*Stow Hill*
Pen-y-clawdd	M	SO 310 201	*Crucorney*
Pencoed[18]	S	ST 406 894	*Langstone*
Penhow	S	ST 425 908	*Penhow; private home*
Penrhos	M	SO 410 132	*Llantilio Crossenny*
*Raglan (176)	S	SO 414 083	*Raglan*

Rockfield F'm Motte	R	SO 424 011	*Llangwm; ringwork despite title RC*
St Illtyd's Castle[19]	M	SO 217 019	Llanhilleth; aka Twyn Motte
*Skenfrith (180)	S	ST 457 203	*Llangattock-vibon-avel*
Trecastle	M	SO 452 070	*Raglan*
Tre-grug	M	ST 370 974	*Llangybi*
Tump Terrett	M	SO 500 054	*Trelleck United; aka Trelleck Castle*
Twmbarlwm	M	ST 244 927	*Risca*
Twyn Tudur	M	ST 193 938	*Ynysddu; aka Mynydd Islwyn*
Twynycregyn	M	SO 363 096	*Llanarth*
*Usk (186)	S	SO 377 010	*Usk*
Wentloog	M	ST 251 834	*Marshfield; aka Castleton*
Wern-y-cwrt	M	SO 394 088	*Llanarth*
*White Castle (180)	S	SO 379 168	*Llantilio Crossenny*

Montgomeryshire

Castle Name		Grid	Notes
Bishop's Moat	M	SO 291 896	*Churchstoke*
Bronfelen	M	SO 052 913	*Llandinam*
Bryn Derwen	M	SO 163 952	*Llandyssil*
Caer Siac	M	SO 129 972	*Bettws; aka Betws Cedewain*
Cann Office Hotel Mound	M	SJ 011 107	*Banwy*
Carreghofa	S	SJ 255 222	*Llanymynech*

Castle Caereinion	M	SJ 163 055	*Castell Caereinion*
Cefn Brytalch	M	SO 175 963	*Llandyssil*
Cefn-coch	M	SJ 105 263	*Llanrhaeadr-ym-Mochnant*
*Dolforwyn (189)	S	SO 152 950	*Llandyssil; W*
Gro Tump	M	SO 123 922	*Newtown and Llanllwchaearn*
Hen Domen, Montgomery (192)	M	SO 214 980	*Montgomery*
Hen Domen II	M	SO 240 199	*Llansantffraid*
Hyssington	M	SO 314 945	*Churchstoke; aka Castle of Sned*
Lady's Mount	M	SJ 212 063	*Welshpool; in Powis Castle park*
Llanidloes	M	SN 954 844	*Llanidloes*
Llyssun	M	SJ 031 101	*Llanerfyl*
Mathrafal	M	SJ 132 107	*Llangyniew*
Moat Castle	M	SO 147 895	*Kerry*
Moat Castle	M	SJ 114 022	*Manafon*
*Montgomery (196)	S	SO 221 968	*Montgomery*
Middle Park	M	SJ 202 057	*Welshpool*
Min-y-Llyn, Lower	M	SJ 211 010	*Forden*
Nantcribba Castle	S	SJ 237 014	*Forden; 'medieval enclosure' RC*
Neuadd Goch[20]	M	SO 079 878	*Kerry*
Newtown Hall	M	SO 107 914	*Newtown and Llanllwchaearn*
Old Hall Camp	E	SO 206 897	*Kerry; see note[21]*

Penycastell	M	SN 982 886	*Llanidloes Without*
*Powis (196)	S	SJ 215 064	*Welshpool*
Rhos Ddiarbed	M	SO 046 905	*Llandinam*
Rhydyronnen	M	SN 923 822	*Llangurig*
Rhysnant Hall Castle	R	SJ 256 175	*Llandrinio*
Simon's Castle	M	SO 285 933	*Churchstoke*
Tomen Buddugre	M	SO 101 696	*Llanddewi Ystradenni*
Tomen Fawr	M	SH 891 026	*Llanbrynmair; aka Tafolwern; W*
Tomen Gastell I	M	SJ 186 202	*Llanfechain*
Tomen Gastell II	M	SJ294 167	*Llandrinio*
Tomen Madoc	M	SO 146 908	*Kerry*
Tomen-y-cefnlloer	M	SJ 119 225	*Llanfyllin; aka Tomen Moelfrochas*
Tomen-yr-allt	M	SJ 127 211	*Llanfyllin*
Upper Luggy	M	SJ 199 021	*Berriew*
Welshpool	M	SJ 230 741	*Welshpool; aka Domen Gastell*

Pembrokeshire

Castle Name		Grid	Notes
Amroth	M	SN 163 077	*Amroth; aka Castle Park*
Benton	S	SN 005 069	*Burton*
Camrose	M	SM 926 198	*Camrose*
*Carew (199)	S	SN 045 037	*Carew*
Castell Blaenllechog	R	SN 110 280	*Mynachlog-ddu; aka Pengawsai*
Castell Cynon	R	SN 155 146	*Lampeter Velfrey*
Castell Crychydd	R	SN 261 348	*Clydau*
Castell Haidd/ Hayscastle	M	SM 895 257	*Hayscastle*
Castell Llainfawr	M	SN 151 374	*Eglwyswrw*
Castell Mael	R	SN 009 297	*Puncheston*
Castlemartin	E	SR 915 984	*Castlemartin; ?reused hill-fort*
Castle Pill	M	SM 919 064	*Milford Haven; aka Blackbridge*
Castlebythe	M	SN 022 290	*Puncheston*
*Cilgerran (202)	S	SN 195 431	*Cilgerran*
Dale	S	SM 805 508	*Dale; mostly 19thC*
Dingstopple	M	SN 061 186	*Llawhaden*
Drim Castle	R	SN 014 196	*Some uncertainty as to function RC*
Eglwyswrw	R	SN 139 383	*Eglwyswrw*
Green Castle	M	SN 128 142	*Narberth; aka Clyn Pattel*
*Haverfordwest (205)	S	SM 943 157	*Haverfordwest*
Henry's Moat	M	SN 044 275	*Puncheston*

Llanfyrnach	M	SN 219 312	Crymych
Llangwathen	M	SN 134 153	Lampeter Felfrey
*Llawhaden (207)	S	SN 013 176	Llawhaden
*Manorbier (209)	S	SO 064 978	Manorbier
*Narberth (211)	S	SN 110 144	Narberth
Nevern	S	SN 083 402	Nevern
New Moat	M	SN 063 253	New Moat
Newport	S	SN 057 388	Newport; private home
Parc Castell	E	SM 941 367	Scleddau
Parcycastell	R	SM 744 252	St David's & the Cathedral Close
Parcydomen	M	SN 175 352	Crymych; aka Dyffryn Mawr
*Pembroke (213)	S	SM 982 016	Pembroke
Pen-yr-allt	R	SN 158 420	Cilgerran
*Picton (218)	S	SN 011 134	Slebech
Pointz	M	SM 830 237	Brawdy; aka Punch Castle
Roch	S	SM 881 212	Nolton & Roch; holiday rental
Rudbaxton Mount	M	SM 960 820	Rudbaxton
Rudbaxton Rath	R	SM 985 188	Rudbaxton; ringwork within Iron Age hill-fort
St Ishmael's Tump	M	SM 835 076	St Ishmaels
Sentence	R	SN 110 116	Templeton
*Tenby (220)	S	SN 138 005	Tenby
Upton	S	SN 021 047	Cosheston; private residence; limited access
Walwyn's Castle	R	SM 872 110	Walwyns Castle
*Wiston (222)	S	SN 022 181	Wiston
Wolfscastle	M	SM 958 265	Wolfscastle

Radnorshire

Castle Name		Grid	Notes
Aberedw I	S	SO 076 473	*Aberedw*
Aberedw II	M	SO 078 471	*Aberedw; aka Pen Garreg Wood*
Barland	M	SO 281 618	*Old Radnor*
Bleddfa	S	SO 209 682	*Llangunllo; stonework almost vanished*
Bogs Mount	M	SO 275 611	*Old Radnor; aka Burfa*
Brynllwyd	M	SO 116 543	*Glascwm; aka Glan Edw; The Mount*
Bryn y Castell	M	SO 290 722	*Knighton*
Buddugre	M	SO 100 696	*Llanddewi Ystradenny*
Castell Caemaerdy	M	SO 034 530	*Llanelwedd; aka Cefn Dyrys*
Castell Foelallt	M	SO 259 676	*Whitton*
Castell Tinboeth	S	SO 090 755	*Llanbadarn Fynydd; perhaps on hill-fort site*
Castell y Blaidd	M	SO 125 798	*Llanbadarn Fynydd*
Castle Nimble	M	SO 248 594	*Old Radnor*
Cefnllys	S	SO 088 614	*Penybont; 2 castles on same ridge*
Cefnllys (Oldcastle)	M	SO 092 630	*Penybont; aka Dinieithon Remfry*
Clyro	M	SO 214 436	*Clyro*
Cnwclas/Knucklas	S	SO 250 745	*Beguildy*
Colwyn Castle	R	SO 108 540	*Glascwm; within Roman fort*
Court/Cwrt Evan Gwynne	M	SO 216 447	*Clyro; aka Castle Kinsey; ?W*

Crugerydd	M	SO 158 593	New Radnor; aka Crugeryr; W
Cymaron	M	SO 152 703	Llanddewi Ystradenny
Dolbedwyn	M	SO 205 491	Gladestry ?Motte ?Bronze Age
Dunn's Lane	M	SO 266 625	Old Radnor
Fforest Wood	M	SO 101 529	Glascwm
Glasbury	M	SO 175 391	Glasbury
Kinnerton	M	SO 245 630	Old Radnor
Knighton	M	SO 284 722	Knighton; degraded and overbuilt
Llandeilo Graban	M	SO 125 449	Painscastle
Llowes	M	SO 190 406	Glasbury; aka Castle Tump
*New Radnor (223)	E	SO 216 610	New Radnor
Norton	M	SO 304 673	Presteigne
*Painscastle[22] (225)	S	SO 166 462	Painscastle; stonework has vanished
Penarth Mount	M	SO 123 526	Glascwm; aka Cenarth
Presteigne	M	SO 310 645	Presteigne
Rhaeadr I	M	SN 967 678	Rhayader; aka Llansantffraid; W
Rhaeadr II	E	SN 968 680	Rhayader
Stanage	M	SO 331 730	Knighton
Tomen Castle	M	SO 172 589	New Radnor; aka Cae-banal
Wormanston	M	SO 268 606	Old Radnor

APPENDIX B

POSSIBLE, POST-MEDIEVAL AND LOST CASTLES

Anglesey

Aberffraw (SH 354 689). Possible motte site (RC).

Castell Trefadog (SH 291 859). Defended enclosure (RC).

Castell Crwn (SH 331 908).

Ynys Cefni (SH 461 743). 'Possible motte site' (RC).

Breconshire

Aberyscir (SO 001 298). Remfry's suggestion (p.99) not confirmed by RC.

Clawdd Brythonig/British (SN 862 369). Not confirmed as a castle by RC.

Crickadarn (SO 088 421). A defended enclosure of possibly medieval date (RC).

Fforest Castle (SN 919 520). Aka Twdin, Caer Aeron; defended enclosure (RC).

Hen Castell (SO 213 166). A possible castle site.

Llanafan Fawr (SN 966 557). Defended enclosure of unknown date (RC).

Llanddew (SO 055 307). Sometimes defined as castle, sometimes as bishop's palace.

Scethrog Castle (SO 104 248). 'Post medieval mansion' (RC).

Talgarth (SO 154 337). A fourteenth-century tower house.

Caernarfonshire

Bryn Bras (SH 545 624). Built 1828–35, architect Thomas Hopper.

Dolwyddelan (SH 721 530). Earthwork not confirmed by RC as medieval.

Gwydir Castle (SH 796 610). Sixteenth-/seventeenth-century dwelling house.

Llanddeiniolen (SH 569 655). Possible motte, though date unknown (RC).

Nefyn (SH 306 405). Earthwork not confirmed by RC as medieval.

Penrhyn (SH 602 719). Victorian millionaire's fantasy by Thomas Hopper. NT.

Tomen Fawr (SH 454 376). RC is uncertain of this site.

Twthill (SH 482 630). 'May have been a motte and bailey' (RC).

Cardiganshire

Castell Cadwgan. Lost to beach erosion. May have been Iron Age.

Castell Pridd (SN 295 403). Motte removed in 1930, but farm name survives.

Dol-wlff (SN 520 445). Earthworks have been entirely removed.

Goginan (SN 690 817). Has disappeared.

Felin Cwrws (SN 351 411). Could equally well be medieval or prehistoric.

Nantyrarian (SN 688 818). Motte destroyed *c.* 1840.

Penycastell (SN 663 674). Earthworks 'sometimes identified as a medieval motte' (RCAHM).

Temple Bar (SN 533 544). This earthwork (Cwmere) is of unknown date.

Carmarthenshire

Baglan (SS 756 923). 'Stone castle' (King); 'Iron Age enclosure' (RC).

Castell Moel (SN 396 165) aka Greencastle. Not medieval nor yet a castle (RC).

Castle Cossan SN 202 268. A mound of unknown date (RC).

Garn Fawr (SN 396 238). 'Earthwork of uncertain date' (RC).

Llanelli Old Castle (SN 500 003). Now in reservoir.

Myddfai (SN 820 310). King saw a motte; RC favours Roman status.

Pant-glas (SN 422 260). A small platform of possibly medieval date (RC).

Rhyd-y-gors. Exact site uncertain, destroyed by railway building.

Denbighshire

Bodelwyddan (SH 998 748). A fantasy begun in 1830, trust-owned.

Bryneuryn Motte (SH 832 798). 'A major dwelling' (RC); not a castle.

Bryn-Ffanigl (SH 921 743). RC is dubious.

Cadwgan Hall (SJ 298 487). Rejected by most authorities.

Ednyfed's Castle. A phantom pursued to no conclusion on *Castles of Wales* website www.castlewales.com.

Gwrych Castle (SH 928 774). A huge 1815 fantasy construction.

Flintshire

Bodelwyddan Castle (SH 998 748). Post-medieval (RC).

Overton Castle (SJ 356434). Vanished stone castle.

Glamorgan

Aberafan (SS 762 901). Vanished stone castle (Davis). 'Built over' (RCAHM).

Beaupre (ST 009 720). Medieval/early modern manor house.

Briton Ferry (SS 731 940). Excavated earthwork, probably Welsh-built castle.

Cae Burdydd (SO 047 102). Aka Vaynor; 'motte' King; burial place (RC).

Candleston Castle (SS 871 772). A massive fortified manor house.

Cefn Mabli (ST 223 840). Listed as possibility by Salter. Not recognised by RC.

Coed-y-cwm (ST 177 689). 'Medieval fortified enclosure' (RC).

Cil Ifor (SS 505 923). Claimed as a castle, is an Iron Age fort (RC).

Cwrt-y-Vil (ST 178 702). Listed by Salter (p.75). Possibly a monastic grange (RC).

Cyfarthfa Castle (SO 041 073). Built 1824; home for William Crawshay II.

Gelli-garn (SS 960 786). A possible motte and bailey (RC).

Granville's Castle, Neath. Site only known approximately (SS 74 97).

Hen Gastell (SS 731 939). Site destroyed by road-building.

Llandaff (ST 156 780). Castle-like, but actually a bishop's palace.

Llanfaches (ST 433 920). Vanished.

Llangewydd (SS 870 810). Destroyed by quarrying.

North Hill Tor (SS 453 938). 'Ringwork' (King); ?Iron Age (RC).

Norton Camp (SS 491 867). 'Ringwork' (King); ?Iron Age (RC).

Oldcastle upon Alun (SS 911 747). Possible castle site (RC).

Pancross enclosure (ST 046 570). A possible castle site (RC).

Penarth Motte (ST 189 716). Built in 1983 to celebrate the Year of the Castle.

Peterston (ST 083 764). Virtually destroyed by bungalows (RC).

Ruperra (ST 219 863). Ruins of 16C house and 19C castellated mansion.

St Nicholas (ST 084 747). 'Defended enclosure' (RC).

St Mary Hill (967 790). Defended enclosure of unknown date (RC).

Scurlage (ST 463 882) Fortified house (RC). Aka Cheriton, Landimore.

Treoda (ST 156 804). Excavated before being built over.

Trecastle (ST 016 814). A fortified manor house, aka Scurlage Castle.

Tŷ-du (ST 046 770). A ditched mound, possibly of post-medieval date (RC).

Merionethshire

Cymer (SH 732 195).[23] Recorded in 1116; present-day mound may be a garden feature (RC).

Deudraeth (SH 586 371).[24]

Erw'r Castell (SH 577 241). Despite name, RC sees no remains.

Garth Rhiwaedog (SH 950 350). May be natural or artificial (RC).

Llanelltyd (SH 732 195). 'Motte' (King); post-medieval (RC).

Tomen-y-castell (SH 950 372). 'Motte' (King), 'post-medieval? (RC).

Monmouthshire

Bishton Castle (??392 880). 'Allegedly the site of Bishton

Castle' (RC).

Bryngwyn (SO 394 088). 'Motte' (King), but see note.[25]

Caer Licyn (SO 390 927). Date and type of monument uncertain (RC).

Cae Wall Wood (ST 403 891). RC queries the motte status of this earthwork.

Chepstow Park (ST 490 979). Date and type of monument uncertain (RC).

Crucorney Fawr (SO 330 218). 'Motte (King); not known to RC.

Goytre Wood (SO 354 233). Date and type of monument uncertain (RC).

Llanbadoc (SO 375 000). 'Ringwork' (King); Iron Age (RC).

Llanvaches (ST 433 920). Probably a mansion ruin (RC).

Madoc's Castle (ST 433 920). Despite name, actually a manorial ruin (RC).

Maindy Hill Camp (ST 302 858). Entirely built over; status ambiguous.

Panteg (ST 311 911). Motte?; 'post-medieval prospect mound' (RC).

Pool Head (ST 403 891). 'Possible motte' (RC).

St Mellon's (ST 227 803). 'Ringwork' (King); unknown to RC.

Trefeddw (SO 330 217). A mound of uncertain status, aka 'The Moat'.

Trostrey (SO 360 043).[26]

Wern-y-cwrt (SO 394 088). A possible motte, but date uncertain (RC).

Montgomeryshire

Llandyssil Bridge (SO 190 957). A mound of unknown date and function (RC).

Pembrokeshire

Angle (SM 866 030). 'Castle' (O.S.); 'uncertain' (RC).

Bonville's Castle (SN 125 052). 'Strong house' (King).

Boulston (SM 981 124). A domestic ruin rather than a castle (RC).

Caldey Island (SN 141 963). The Prior's Tower is often claimed as a castle.

Castell Mael (SN 009 298). Aka Puncheston; uncertain date (RC).

Castell Poeth (SM 897 377). 'Defended enclosure' (RC).

Castell-y-Fran (SN 081 222). 'No longer accepted as a motte' (RC).

Castlemartin (SR 915 984). ?Iron Age, possibly reused as castle (RC).

Castle Morris (SM 903 316). Lost castle.

Cresswell (SN 049 070). 'Sham castle' or fortified house built early 17C.[27]

Hean Castle I (SN 138 059). Not known to RC.[28]

Hean Castle II (SN 138 059). 19C stone mansion (RC).

Letterston (SM 938 295). A motte or round barrow entirely removed.

Little Newcastle (SM 980 289). 'Motte & bailey removed 1965' (Salter).

Manian Fawr (SN 150 479). A defended enclosure of uncertain date (RC).

Manorowen (SM 942 367). A defended enclosure, possibly of medieval date (RC).

Minwear (SN 062 135). '?Iron Age (RC); 'ringwork' (King).

Newhouse (SN 072 136). Aka Castell Coch, actually a fortified house.

Newport Old Castle (SN 058 396). 'Defended enclosure of unknown date' (RC).

Pantycadno (SN 112 226). Enclosure of uncertain date (RC).

Parc Moat (SM 938 295). King's 'motte' is RC's 'round barrow of unknown age'.

Parc-y-marl (SN 047 245). Enclosure perhaps of Iron Age date (RC).

Picton II (SN 016 135). 'A belvedere or prospect mound' (RC).

Stackpole (SR 977 961). The demolished mansion was originally a medieval castle.

Radnorshire

Boughrood Castle (SO 132390). King's 'motte' unknown to RC.

Castell y Blaidd (SO 124 797). 'Defended enclosure, age uncertain' (RC).

Castell Caemardy (SO 035 531). Date unknown (RCAHM).

Cefn Llech (SN 961 771). A defended enclosure, date unknown (RC).[29]

Cwrt Evan Glyn (SO 215 447). RCAHM offers several interpretations.

Discoed (SO 277 648). Various interpretations have been offered for this mound.

Evancoyd (SO 261 632). King's 'motte' is RC's probable 'garden feature'.

Evenjobb (SO 263 624). 'Period unknown. ?Motte' (RC).

Gwaunceste (SO 156 568). Round barrow (RC).

Old Radnor (SO 250 590). Defended enclosure, possibly medieval (RC).

Rhaeadr (SN 968 680). 'No visible remains' RC. Welsh.

ENDNOTES

1. This book is much indebted to Robert Liddiard's *Castles in Context: Power, Symbolism and Landscape, 1066 to 1500* (Windgather Press, 2005), which sets out an interpretation of medieval castles in terms of their political, social and environmental impact as well as military function.

2. *Sir Cleges*; *Geraint ac Enid*.

3. Anglesey is an anomaly, having so few castles: 1 motte and 1 stone castle are definite. COFLEIN names two possible ringworks but does not mention that said by DJ Cathcart King to be at Llanfaethlu (see Appendix A below).

4. Aka Rhyd-y-briw, Sennybridge. See King, *Brycheiniog XXI*, 1984/5, pp.9–13.

5. Described by RC under Waun Gunllwch as a defended enclosure, but by King as 'a very fine specimen of its type', i.e. a half-ringwork (*Brycheiniog VII*, 1961, p.87).

6. Access (fee-paying) is through the splendid 14C manor house.

7. RC is not convinced that this earthwork is medieval, but its identification with the known existence of a medieval castle seems reasonable.

8. A fine Iron Age hill-fort has been cut in two by a massive ditch. Despite the opinion of RC, I am convinced that the ditch was dug to make a castle of the northern half.

9. This name leads to confusion with the nearby castellated 19C mansion of Glandyfi. Tomen Las is also known as Abereinon.

10. Built on the site of an Iron Age promontory fort.

11. Traditionally associated with Gwenllian, daughter of Llywelyn the Great, wife of William de Lacy (RC). RC seems suspicious of a medieval date, but describes it as a motte-and-bailey, as does OS.

12. Although COFLEIN refers to this as a 'prospect mound', its detailed record gives a medieval/post medieval date, and implies that what was a motte (the word is never used) was

taken over for landscape purposes.

[13] Anglo-Norman ringwork on site of early medieval (6-8 C) Welsh defended site.

[14] Site typically Welsh, within Welsh lordship of Senghennydd; stonework perhaps later English.

[15] Defined by RC as a motte and bailey although the medieval date is queried.

[16] 'Traditional site of palace of kings of Over Gwent' (RC).

[17] Defined by RC as a motte although the medieval date is queried.

[18] Some remains of castle; largely rebuilt as manor house.

[19] Defined by RC as a motte although the medieval date is queried.

[20] Defined by RC as a motte although the medieval date is queried.

[21] Although said by RC to be of unknown date, it is acknowledged that this unfinished enclosure may be the abandoned castle recorded as Hubert's Folly.

[22] Has the aliases Llanbedr and, delightfully, Garde Doloureuse.

[23] Castle recorded in 1116; present-day mound may be a garden feature (RC).

[24] Deudraeth is a modern castellated building near an early site, mentioned by Gerald of Wales; no trace is currently visible.

[25] If this is the same as RCAHM's SO 391078, their opinion is 'Iron Age; Roman'.

[26] 'Possible remains of 11th century manorial hall and circa A.D. 950 pre-Norman round house.' (RC).

[27] Best authority is *Pembrokeshire* (Lloyd, Orbach & Scourfield; 'Pevsner' Buildings of Wales), attributing it to William Barlow (d. 1676), not the earlier bishop of St David's of the same name.

[28] The picture on p.110 of Lise Hull's *Castles and Bishops' Palaces of Pembrokeshire* looks remarkably like a motte.

[29] Remfry lists this site as 'low-lying earthworks', possibly 13C, under the names Cwm y Saeson or Dulas.

INDEX OF CASTLES